# Date Due

| FEB 26 | | | |
|--------|--|--|--|
| MAR 12 | | | |
| NOV 22 | | | |
| | | | |
| DEC 6 | | | |
| MAR 13 | | | |
| MAR 27 | | | |
| JAN 19 | | | |
| APR 24 | | | |
| MAY 15 | | | |
| JAN 11 | | | |
| | | | |
| MAR 14 | | | |
| DEC 8 | | | |
| | | | |
| DEC 13 | | | |
| MAY 23 | | | |
| MAY 29 | | | |
| JUL 28 | | | |
| MAY 23 | | | |
| MAY 9 | | | |
| | | | |
| | | | |
| | | | |
| No. 293 | DEMCO-MADISON-WIS | | |

# SOCIAL PROBLEMS OF CHILDHOOD

THE MACMILLAN COMPANY
NEW YORK · BOSTON · CHICAGO · DALLAS
ATLANTA · SAN FRANCISCO

MACMILLAN & CO., LIMITED
LONDON · BOMBAY · CALCUTTA
MELBOURNE

THE MACMILLAN COMPANY
OF CANADA, LIMITED
TORONTO

# SOCIAL PROBLEMS
# OF CHILDHOOD

### By PAUL HANLY FURFEY

*of the Department of Sociology*
*Catholic University of America*

NEW YORK
## THE MACMILLAN COMPANY
### 1929

PRINTED IN THE UNITED STATES OF AMERICA
BY THE STRATFORD PRESS, INC.

25731

TO
WILLIAM J. KERBY,
WHOSE UNFAILING INTEREST AND ENCOURAGEMENT
HAVE MADE THIS BOOK POSSIBLE

# PREFACE

Childhood has always had its social problems, but they were never more acute than in our present complex and constantly shifting civilization. At the same time science has supplied us with new techniques with which to meet these problems. Out of these new needs and new resources a new attitude toward the child and his difficulties has been developed. The purpose of this book is to give an account of the community's attack on the social problems of childhood in the light of this new attitude.

Various influences mould the growing child. Some of these influences affect his body, some his mind, some his character. Some are operative at home, some outside of the home. Among all these influences, Religion stands paramount. The present writer cannot too strongly stress his conviction—shared by all Catholics—that the neglect of the teachings of Christ is a supremely important factor underlying all social problems. Until these principles are recognized and put into practice there can be no funda-

mentally satisfactory cure for our social ills. A
thorough solution for the social problems of
childhood must be sought in the doctrines of
Christ.

The purpose of the present book, however,
is not to examine the rôle of the Church in social
work, but to examine the rôle of the State. In
the Middle Ages when the whole civilized
world professed one Faith it was possible for
the Church to assume the actual administration
of practically all social projects. Under modern
conditions this is no longer feasible. The burden of social-welfare work is borne partly by
religious bodies, partly by other private organizations, and partly by the community as a whole.
In this volume the writer will treat of the community's share in the solution of the problems
of childhood, reserving the treatment of the
Church's activities to a future work.

The purpose is to set before all who are interested in children's welfare the content of the
new social and scientific work which is so helpful in the understanding of child life under
present conditions. The child must be dealt with
always as a spiritual being. The author believes
that those who are concerned with the complete welfare of the child will gain insight and
wisdom if they take account of the knowledge

and experience that social research has made
available. Public authorities are doing much
that is of great value. Our problem is to maintain Christian philosophy always and to relate
public activity to it as far as possible. Thus, for
instance, juvenile delinquency is a moral and
spiritual problem. As such it concerns our religious teachers profoundly. But social work and
juvenile courts have gained profound insight
into the sociological backgrounds of delinquency. Consequently the author believes that
our religious teachers are concerned with the
experience and administration of juvenile
courts. Such problems are treated in this volume from the social standpoint only. Those
charged with the religious care of children will
supply in all cases the fundamental spiritual
element demanded in any complete view of this
or any other problem.

Gratitude is due to many persons whose assistance has made the preparation of this book
a pleasant task. Various members of the staff
of the United States Children's Bureau gave
generously of their time, reading the manu-
script of certain chapters and aiding the author
immeasurably by their suggestions. Dr. James
F. Rogers of the United States Bureau of Education assisted by helpful criticism of Chapter

III and Mr. Paul Komora of the staff of the
National Committee for Mental Hygiene gave
similar help with Chapter V. Dr. George L.
Wallace, Superintendent of the Wrentham
State School, Wrentham, Massachusetts, read
the proof of Chapter VII. While these persons
helped very greatly in the preparation of this
book, they cannot be held responsible for any
mistakes which may appear. The author must
accept full responsibility for these.

PAUL HANLY FURFEY.

# CONTENTS

# SOCIAL PROBLEMS OF CHILDHOOD

# SOCIAL PROBLEMS OF CHILDHOOD

## CHAPTER I

### *The Child and the Community*

It is a trite observation that our age is a time of remarkable progress. As long as civilization endures, the Twentieth Century will be celebrated as the century in which man first learned to fly and to communicate without wires. Everyone realizes that our generation has won extraordinary victories in the field of physical science, but probably fewer realize that its achievements in the social sciences have been scarcely less striking. The vast and fundamental social changes of our day are less obvious than the achievements of applied physical science, yet they have an even more intimate relation to the course of our lives.

Among these recent developments some of the most striking belong to the field of child welfare. During the present century the State has

1

taken a more intimate and effective interest in the well-being of the child than ever before. Public-health work has succeeded in adding several years to the child's life. The juvenile-court movement and mental hygiene have helped to combat disorders of conduct. A totally new conception of public relief work has succeeded in preventing much child dependency and in treating the remainder in a more humane and wiser manner. An altogether changed conception of the school has brought it into closer relationship with life and has been preparing the child for his vocation in a more adequate manner. Altogether the newer interest of the State in the social problems of childhood constitutes a most remarkable chapter in the Twentieth Century's story of achievement.

A few observers have seen in this recent movement a tendency towards State paternalism. It would be unfortunate indeed if this fear were justified. When the State kills individual initiative it destroys one of man's choicest prerogatives. But a closer examination of the movement appears to show no grounds for such a fear. Indeed, there is nothing in modern child-welfare work which was not anticipated, at least in germ, in long-standing legal tradition. A distinctive thing about American child-welfare work is its fundamental conservatism. The recent advances in this field have been due not so much to a changed conception of the State's responsibility as to a revolutionary increase in the efficiency of its welfare work.

The conception of the State's responsibility towards those in need of special care has a venerable history in English tradition. The problem became acute at the time of the Reformation. Before that, the work had been under the care of the Church but when the State confiscated the Church's property it was forced to accept the latter's responsibility towards the indigent as well. The Tudor period was a time of experimentation which finally culminated in the Poor Relief Act of 1601 (43 Elizabeth c. 2). This was passed as a more or less temporary measure but with some slight modification it remained in force throughout the whole Seventeenth Century and continued to serve as the basis of legislation long after that time.

English practice furnished the background of American public welfare work. Indeed the very terminology of English law was often adopted without modification. We find, therefore, in the Colonial period that welfare work was made a responsibility of the local administrative unit throughout the country with very little attempt to supervise or control the work on the part of the government of the Colonies. Moreover, the methods found in English charitable work were carefully reproduced here and the almshouse and outdoor relief were the two ways of relieving the indigent in Colonial America.

It was not long before the inadequacy of this system became apparent. Some towns and counties had neither the financial resources nor the experience in administration necessary for efficient welfare work. As early as 1767 Massachusetts passed an act by which the State was given the duty of removing from its confines indigent persons who had no legal residence there. A much more significant acknowledgment of the State's responsibility was the establishment by Virginia in 1769 of a State institution for the insane. Pennsylvania founded a State Prison in 1790. During the first half of the Nineteenth Century this movement progressed rapidly and institutions for the insane, feeble-minded, deaf, and criminal were opened throughout the United States (3).

The efficiency of the institutions controlled by the states as contrasted with the backwardness of those managed by town and county authorities impressed thoughtful persons. Many felt that there should be a still further centralization and that the Federal Government should play a large part in welfare work. Any direct control was rendered impossible by constitutional limitations, but there remained the possibility of indirect coöperation through federal grants to the states. This possibility was brought sharply to the attention of the public by the eloquent appeal of Miss Dorothea Dix for federal aid in the care of the insane and deaf. The measure was passed by Congress but was vetoed by President Pierce in 1854. Since that time public provision for dependent, defective, and delinquent children has been recognized as a function of state and local governments.

The early state institutions acted as independent units. Each was controlled by its own board of directors and there was little attempt to centralize them under some state agency. The evils of this system soon became apparent. It was realized that some sort of central supervision was necessary. The Massachusetts Board of State Charities was authorized by the Legislature of 1863. Four years later Ohio and New York took similar action and from that time to the present there has been a constantly increasing centralization of state welfare work.

In spite of the extent of state supervision the actual operation of American welfare work traditionally is a rather local affair. This is due partly to the influence of the English Poor Law system which was taken over almost bodily by the colonists and partly to the genius of American government which has always favored the local unit of administration in contrast to the highly centralized government, for example, of France or Italy. This tendency to make welfare work a local responsibility has been modified only where it has proved strikingly inefficient. Most of the work reviewed in succeeding chapters of this volume is organized on a local basis.

The state government supplements the work of the local government in three ways. First, it defines the exact powers of the local units of administration by legislation. Secondly, by supervisory and educational activities it endeavors to obtain a uniform high standard of work throughout the state. Thirdly, it organizes and administers projects too large or too difficult for the city or town—projects such as statewide child placement, or institutions for the insane, delinquent, epileptic, deaf, or feeble-minded.

The Federal Government attempts no direct welfare work except in the territories and agencies under immediate federal jurisdiction. But it plays a most important part in the solution of social problems by its research work and by setting up standards as guides for state and local governments and private agencies. In only a few instances has it attempted to induce the states to follow specific standards by offers of federal aid to those who accept them.

Since the local unit of government plays the largest part in child-welfare work, and since social problems are more acute in our crowded centers of population, social work of all sorts has been brought to its highest stage of development in the cities. The form of administrative organization of municipal welfare work shows a very great variety because the form of city government is itself highly unstandardized in this country. A great deal depends upon the amount of freedom allowed to the cities by the state legislature. Much depends also on the form of city government. The old mayor-and-council plan favored decentralized authority and welfare work was generally organized under a number of rather unrelated agencies. The newer plan of city government by a commission, which originated at Galveston in 1901—and still more the city-manager plan which originated in Sumter, South Carolina, in 1913—favors a more centralized control not only in the city government as a whole but in each separate department (14). Many of the social problems of childhood treated in this book are handled by the city through its departments dealing with health, education, delinquency, dependency, and recreation. A few words must be devoted to each of these.

There are two opposite tendencies in city health administration. Either the department of health is under the control of an administrative appointive board, usually unpaid, or else it is centralized under a single executive head. The United States Public Health Service survey (23) of practices in 1923 in the 100 largest cities in the United States showed the former arrangement in 43 cities and the latter in 32. In 18 more cities the department head was under the more or less nominal control of an *ex-officio* board and in seven others he worked with an advisory board. Organization of health activities under an administrative board represents the older tendency and is more frequently associated with the mayor-and-council type of government while the newer types favor control by single administrative heads.

Of the problems treated in this book the city health department usually is responsible for the maternal and infant health work. This is often organized under a division of child hygiene in the health department. In a number of cities also the health department is responsible for the school medical inspection. The Public Health Service survey showed that this was the case in 23 out of 98 large cities while in 18 the health and school departments coöperated in this work. A survey by the American Child Health Association (2) showed that school medical inspection was carried on by the health department in 22 out of 86 small cities.

Since the school is the one agency which reaches nearly all the children of the city it is not surprising to find that it plays a large part in the solution of the problems treated in this volume. Vocational guidance and placement, the issuing of work certificates, and the training of the feeble-minded outside institutions are commonly associated with the schools. As has been said above, school medical inspection is most frequently carried on under the administrative control of the educational authorities. This was true in 57 out of 98 larger cities covered by the Public Health survey and in 55 out of 86 smaller cities studied by the American Child Health Association. In most cities the schools give at least some sort of elementary health instruction. More recently they are beginning to take an interest in mental hygiene, through the school psychologist and occasionally through the school clinic. The work of the visiting teacher and of the progressive attendance departments marks the entrance of the school into the field of social service. The administration of city public-school systems is fairly well standardized in this country and is normally organized under an administrative board of education working through a superintendent of schools.

The city may or may not be directly responsible for the treatment of juvenile delinquency; for the juvenile court may be either one of the municipal courts or it may be a district or county court and therefore exempt from municipal control. The latter plan is theoretically preferable and more common in practice. Consequently the tendency is in the direction of the control of juvenile delinquency by some administrative unit larger than the city.

Problems of social inadequacy including poverty, unemployment, dependency, and so forth have been subject to a number of sorts of control. Frequently relief work is regarded as a county function and the city has no responsibility in this field. Where it is regarded as a function of the city, municipal practice has passed through three distinct periods. When this work first developed each type of service was under a different head. An overseer of the poor was responsible for outdoor relief, the poorhouse was controlled by a superintendent and board of trustees, and so forth. As the need of uniform work became evident these various agencies were organized into a single department under an administrative board. Finally the latest arrangement found at least in the largest cities is control by a single man under the title of superintendent of public welfare or some similar designation (6 and 15). The problem of child dependency is the chief problem of childhood to be met by such a department.

A final function of city government in regard to children is the provision of adequate recreation. Three municipal agencies have been responsible for this work at different times and places—the school board, the park department, and a special recreation commission. The present tendency seems to be to make all organized recreation work among school children a function of the school department and to coördinate it closely with the physical-education work of the schools while the balance of the municipal recreation program is organized under a special department with a superintendent at the head of it who is responsible to an administrative recreation commission (17).

The country has lagged behind the city in the matter of welfare work. This was partly due to the fact that social problems in general are less acute in rural than in urban districts and partly to the greater efficiency of the more compact city government. In the present century, however, the attention of thoughtful people has been focused on the problems of rural areas as never before. The most common unit of rural welfare work is the county, although the importance of this area varies greatly from New England, where it is overshadowed in importance by the town, to the South and West, where it is the only local area of government. However, the general tendency has been to assign more and more importance to the county (19).

Striking advances have been made in the last ten or fifteen years in the field of general social service in rural areas. The major problem here has been the provision of trained social workers. The present-day ideal is to have at least one such worker in each county carrying on her work, either under a local board or independently of local authority, but aided and supervised by some state department. Her program of activities may be quite general. Besides the usual family case work it may include probation and school attendance work, the investigation of applications for mothers' pensions, and child placement (5, 11, and 22).

Although the exact form of organization has varied greatly from state to state a common feature running through all systems of county welfare work has been the predominant part played by some state agency. The most satisfactory work has been done where the county organization is strong. In some states such as Minnesota, North Carolina, and Virginia, the state has developed a consistent program of child-welfare work in accordance with a well-thought-out plan. Others, such as California and Pennsylvania, have adopted more flexible programs, cooperating with county boards and developing in each county the type of organization which seems best to succeed in the local situation, without attempting to enforce a uniform system throughout the state. Iowa has developed an original system of coöperation between private and public agencies in county work (16). A few states such as New York and Ohio have limited the county organization to the care of dependent children (11).

Rural child-health work has made great progress during the present century. Systematic health work in the country areas began with the appointment of full-time county or district

health officers. Although remarkable progress
has been made in the last two decades, due particularly to the activities of the United States
Public Health Service and the Rockefeller
Foundation, a great deal remains to be done.
Less than one-fifth of our rural population is at
present served by full-time officials (10).

An outstanding piece of rural child-health
work has been the work carried out under the
Federal Maternity and Infancy Act of 1921. By
the terms of this act federal aid was granted to
each state which would undertake a program for
the promotion of the welfare and hygiene of
mothers and young children in accordance with
the provisions of the act. Except for an annual
outright grant of five thousand dollars the states
can obtain Federal funds only if matched by
state appropriations. All except three states have
accepted the benefits of this act. In over four-
fifths of the counties comprised in these states
some maternity and infancy work has been carried out under its provisions. This work includes
maternity and child-health conferences, public-
health nursing, mothers' classes, and general educational work. The act expires June 30, 1929,
and the responsibility of carrying on the activities undertaken will then rest solely with the
states.

In education the situation is somewhat different. For school purposes the unit of local government has been traditionally some area smaller than the county, generally a township or school district. There is, at present, a well defined tendency to consolidate these districts and to grant a larger measure of control to the county superintendent and board of education. The increased efficiency which has followed from this larger administrative unit has been responsible for the introduction into rural areas of many of the modern methods which are usually associated with city school systems. Although the administration of education has thus been a town or county function the state has played an important part by setting standards and by aiding poor districts through equalization funds.

The rôle of the state in welfare work is twofold. It undertakes a certain amount of work directly and it supervises the work of cities and towns and private organizations, endeavoring to educate them to higher standards. The work undertaken directly by the state includes the administration of institutions for various classes of socially inadequate, factory inspection, and in some states, child protection, mental hygiene clinics, and other activities. The work of the state both supervisory and administrative is extremely important. It would not be too much to say that the higher standards which now prevail in public-welfare work are due more to the activity of the state than to any other single cause.

As has been said already, state administration and supervision of welfare work has gone through several stages. The three outstanding forms of organization at present are the departmental form with a strong executive, the professional board with salaried, full-time members, and the lay board. Under the first of these plans the welfare work of the state is centralized into one or more departments, each with a single appointive, administrative head with plenary power. This arrangement secures a maximum of efficiency but is open to the danger of political influence. The professional board is often found where the state undertakes large important administrative functions which in other states would be carried on by boards of managers of separate institutions. Many look upon the lay board with a single responsible executive officer as the best form of state administrative organization. If this board consists of members serving for long terms which expire at different times it should be comparatively free from political influence and if it has the power

to appoint an executive to carry out its policies
it may secure the same degree of efficiency as
would the one-man form of departmental
control.

State commissions for the study and revision
of child-welfare laws have played an important
part in the improvement of state welfare work.
The movement dates from 1911, when the Commission to Codify and Revise the Laws of Ohio
Relative to Children was appointed. Up to the
present 30 states, together with the District of
Columbia and Porto Rico, have appointed such
commissions. Although naturally not all the legislation recommended by them has been passed
they have accomplished much. They have often
succeeded in coördinating and unifying child-
welfare laws as well as in modernizing them
(12). In recent years the tendency has been not
so much to appoint general commissions to codify all the state laws as to appoint special commissions to report on special problems, such, for
instance, as the care of crippled children or the
work of the juvenile court.

On account of constitutional limitations as
well as public opinion the Federal Government
has undertaken little direct welfare work. Attempts have been made to obtain federal control in certain fields, but such attempts have

usually failed, for instance, in the case of the two federal child-labor laws which have been declared unconstitutional. It must not be imagined, however, that the Federal Government has not been active in the field of child welfare. The reverse is certainly true. But the activities of the government have generally taken the form of making surveys, promoting the adoption of minimum standards, and carrying on fundamental research. It is equipped to do these things better than any state government.

The outstanding federal agency in the field of child welfare is the United States Children's Bureau (21), founded in 1912. This agency has published excellent studies on maternal and child hygiene, child labor, dependency, and juvenile delinquency. It administers the Federal Maternity and Infancy Act and for the brief periods when the first federal child-labor law was in force it administered that law as well.

The United States Public Health Service has made studies in the field of child health (4) and coöperated with state health departments in activities of various types. The Federal Board for Vocational Education (7) has been active in promoting vocational education and the rehabilitation of the victims of industrial accidents, both through a system of coöperation with the states. The Department of Agriculture has accomplished excellent work for rural boys and girls particularly through its 4-H clubs. Thus in various ways governmental agencies have aided the cause of child welfare.

The above has dealt with publicly supported child-welfare activities alone. But a very large proportion of such work is being done by private agencies. There are those who feel that social work is a community affair and should be carried on exclusively by the State but a juster view holds that public and private agencies have each a part to play. Public welfare work has the advantage of being backed up by legal authority and therefore it can exercise a control over the person, for instance, in cases of delinquency, which a private agency cannot parallel. The sources of revenue of public work are more certain than those of private work and therefore public agencies are better fitted in the words of Kelso (8) for "those problems fully demonstrated as equitable, practicable, and appropriate for the whole people to deal with out of funds raised by taxation."

Public welfare work has, however, the great disadvantage of being relatively inflexible. Since it is authorized by statute an executive is not able to put into operation new and original plans without further legislation. The function of privately supported welfare work, therefore, is the development of new and original projects in the field of social work, the treatment of those more subtle problems which do not call for direct legislative action, the creation of public opinion in support of the public agency, and the stimulation of the latter to higher standards. Practically all the important recent developments in the social-welfare field have been tried out in the first place by private agencies.

Another field for private initiative is the treatment of religious problems. Since our government is necessarily non-sectarian it cannot be expected to handle difficulties in this field. Religious bodies have accomplished this by coöperation with public agencies or by developing their own institutions for dependents, case work among indigent families, settlements, clubs, day nurseries, and similar ventures. In fact, outside of law enforcement there is scarcely any public activity which is not paralleled by private organizations.

Modern child-welfare work is inspired by the conviction that every child is endowed with certain inalienable rights. He must not be deprived of these rights through an accident of birth. Whether his home be in the crowded section of a great city or in some sparsely settled rural district he has a right to health, to a decent home, to self-development. Through a great broadening of its field and through the standardization of state agencies modern welfare work is gradually bringing it about that every child shall enjoy this natural birthright.

## BIBLIOGRAPHY

(1) American Academy of Political and Social Science: *Public welfare in the United States.* Edited by Howard W. Odum. Philadelphia, The American Academy of Political and Social Science, 1923. vi, 282 p. (Annals of the American Academy of Political and Social Science, Vol. 105.)
Authoritative papers on public welfare organization and its relation to private work.

(2) American Child Health Association, Research Division: *A health survey of 86 cities.* New York, American Child Health Association, 1925. xxxiv, 614 p.
Deals with cities ranging in population from 40,000 to 70,000.

(3) Breckinridge, Sophonisba P.: *Public welfare administration in the United States; select documents.* Chicago, The University of Chicago Press, 1927. xxiii, 786 p.
A collection of source material on this topic.

(4) Clark, Taliaferro: *Some child hygiene activities of the United States Public Health Service.* Washington, D. C., U. S. Gov't Printing Office, 1922. 12 p. (Reprint No. 723 from the Public Health Reports.)
These activities include epidemiological studies,

studies in school hygiene, mental hygiene, child health organization, nutrition, mouth hygiene, and other subjects.

(5) Curry, H. Ida: *Public child-caring work in certain counties of Minnesota, North Carolina, and New York.* Washington, D. C., U. S. Gov't Printing Office, 1927. v., 96 p.  (Children's Bureau Publication No. 173.)

A recent study of county organization.

(6) Dickey, James A.: "Department of public welfare in representative cities." *Annals of the American Academy of Political and Social Science,* 105: 149-50, January, 1923.

Outlines of organization in 14 large cities.

(7) Federal Board for Vocational Education: *Federal Board for Vocational Education. Statement of policies.* Revised edition. Washington, D. C., U. S. Gov't Printing Office, 1927. vi, 107 p.  (Federal Board for Vocational Education, Bulletin No. 1.)

The general aims and principles of this agency.

(8) Kelso, Robert W.: "The relation between public and private enterprises in public welfare service." *Social Forces,* 5: 489-500, March, 1927.

The respective functions of the two sorts of work are compared.

(9) Kelso, Robert W.: *The science of public welfare.* New York, Henry Holt and Company, 1928. xii, 428 p. An excellent treatment of the whole field dealing both with general principles and with practical methods.

(10) Lumsden, L. L.: *Extent of rural health service in the United States* 1924-1928. Washington, D. C., U. S. Gov't Printing Office, 1928. 14 p.  (Reprint No. 1220 from the Public Health Reports.)

Lists counties and districts having whole-time health officers. Only 19.63 per cent of our rural population live in such districts.

(11) Lundberg, Emma O.: *The county as a unit for an organized program of child caring and protective work*. Washington, D. C., U. S. Gov't Printing Office, 1926. iii, 25 p. (Children's Bureau Publication No. 169.)
A summary and revision of reference (22).

(12) Lundberg, Emma O.: *State commissions for the study and revision of child-welfare laws*. Washington, D. C., U. S. Gov't Printing Office, 1924. v, 156 p. (Children's Bureau Publication No. 131.)
Includes references and texts of laws.

(13) Mathews, John Mabry: *American state government*. New York, London, D. Appleton and Company, 1924. xv, 660 p.
A standard work on the subject.

(14) Maxey, Chester C.: *An outline of municipal government*. Garden City, New York, Doubleday, Page & Company, 1924. xvii, 388 p.
Contains a chapter on "Public Welfare."

(15) Mayer, Joseph: "Municipal public welfare administration in a city of 200,000 to 750,000 population." *Journal of Social Forces*, 2:213-20, January, 1924.
Centralized control in a large city. Reprinted in reference (18).

(16) McClenahan, Bessie A.: *The Iowa plan for the combination of public and private relief*. Iowa City, Iowa, The University of Iowa, 1918. 73 p. (University of Iowa Monographs. Studies in the Social Sciences Vol. 5. No. 3.)
An account of this unique coöperative plan.

(17) Nash, Jay B.: *The organization and administration of playgrounds and recreation.* New York, A. S. Barnes & Company, 1927. xii, 547 p.
This standard reference contains an unusually full treatment of the legal status and administrative organization of municipal recreation.

(18) Odum, Howard W. and Willard, D. W.: *Systems of public welfare.* Chapel Hill, University of North Carolina Press, 1925. vi, 302 p.
An excellent summary.

(19) Porter, Kirk H.: *County and township government in the United States.* New York, The Macmillan Company, 1922, xiii, 362 p.
The standard reference on the subject.

(20) Reed, Thomas Harrison: *Municipal government in the United States.* New York, The Century Co., 1926. vii, 378 p.
Discusses some outstanding problems.

(21) Tobey, James A.: *The Children's Bureau; its history, activities and organization.* Baltimore, The Johns Hopkins Press, 1925. xii, 83 p. (Institute for Government Research. Service Monographs of the United States Government No. 21.)
An excellent brief account of this bureau.

(22) U. S. Children's Bureau: *County organization for child care and protection.* Washington, D. C., U. S. Gov't Printing Office, 1922. vii, 173 p. (Children's Bureau Publication No. 107.)
A long study brought up to date by reference (11).

(23) U. S. Public Health Service: *Municipal health department practice for the year* 1923 *based upon surveys of the* 100 *largest cities in the United States made by the United States Public Health Service in coöperation with the Committee on Administrative Practice, American Public Health As-*

*sociation.* Washington, D. C., U. S. Gov't Printing Office, 1926. xxiii, 782 p. (Public Health Bulletin No. 164.)

A very thorough study. Each chapter is written by an expert in the field covered.

(24) Vaile, Gertrude: "An organization problem of public welfare departments." *The Annals of the American Academy of Political and Social Science.* 105:144-48, January, 1923.

Contends that a public welfare department should have a board with powers "more than advisory, but less than administrative."

(25) Wright, Henry Collier: *A valuation of a system for the administration of state institutions through one man control as operated in Illinois, made for the State Charities Aid Association. New York,* United Charities Building, 1922. 48 p.

An impartial view of Illinois' pioneer system.

# CHAPTER II

## *Child Health—The Pre-School Period*

The lengthening of human life has been an outstanding accomplishment of modern public health work. A white baby boy born in the United States Registration Area in 1901 had an expectation of life of 48.23 years. That is to say, the average length of life amounted to that figure. Nineteen years later it had become 54.05 (10). The application of modern medical knowledge had added almost six years to the span of human life during the first two decades of the Twentieth Century.

This increase has been due principally to successful work in the field of child health; for during the same period the expectation of life for white males at the age of 30 had increased only about a year and a half. Accurate figures on infant deaths have been gathered by the United States Census Bureau only since 1915, but we know that the infant mortality for the Registration Area rate has fallen from 99.9 per thousand live births in that year to 64.6, for 1927. Among 26 foreign countries for which comparable statistics for 1925 have been published only six had lower rates than the United States.

It might seem that in view of these facts that we have reason to be proud of our work in behalf of the infant and pre-school child. We have indeed accomplished much, yet there are certain disquieting features which will not permit us any great degree of self-congratulation.

The first of these is our alarming maternal mortality rate. The health of the newborn child is intimately bound up with the health of the mother. It is somewhat alarming therefore to learn that in 1925 there were 647 maternal deaths for each hundred thousand live births in the United States Birth Registration Area. This rate was higher than that of any of 20 foreign countries for which comparable statistics were available.

A second unpleasant fact is that, although we have made wonderful progress in reducing the death rate of infants after the first month, the rate for infants below one month of age has been reduced only slightly. About one-half of the total deaths under one year occur in the first month. Very little has been accomplished with infants of this age.

As has just been stated, the age period comprising the second to the twelfth months of life has been the battlefield upon which public-health work has waged its most successful battle against the slaughter of the innocents; yet careful studies have shown that even here very much more remains to be done. For example, Collins (3) studied the causes of deaths of infants in nine American cities, classifying them into 12 groups. In some of these groups there was remarkably little difference between various cities. Such were the rates for congenital malformations, debility, premature birth, and injuries at birth. But certain other diseases showed surprising variations. For example, the rate for diarrhea and enteritis in Fall River was 10.73 times as great as in Seattle. The rate for the infectious diseases of children was 4.89, and that for bronchitis was 3.50 times as great in the former as in the latter city. Other cities show similar striking variations. The moral to be drawn is that certain diseases not subject to control are rather constant throughout the country, while other diseases, especially the infectious diseases which will respond to proper health measures, vary according to the quality of work being done.

In 1926 the death rate in the Registration Area for the continental United States for white babies between one and twelve months of age was 32.9, while it was 63.8 for negro babies. There is probably little difference in the innate vitality of these two races and we can only ascribe the fact that the negro rate is about twice the white rate to lack of proper public-health work among our large colored population.

A study made by the American Child Health Association (1) of the public-health activities of 86 cities showed that although infant hygiene was receiving a great deal of attention, yet it reached only 58 per cent of the standard set up in the Appraisal Form of the American Public Health Association.

Again, there is much room for improvement in our public-health work for children between their first birthday and the time of entrance into school. This has well been called "the neglected age" of childhood from the standpoint of health work. The above survey of the American Child Health Association (1) showed that pre-school hygiene rated tenth among eleven public health activities in the cities studied and the average score of these cities on the Appraisal Form represented only 32 per cent of the minimum standards.

Studies of the health of pre-school children are largely lacking so that it is difficult to estimate the extent of the problem at this period. But the most careful survey to date, namely the Gary Survey (14), showed that among 4348 children between the the ages of two and seven only 4.8 per cent were entirely free from physical defect.

To understand why our health work among infants and young children has not reached its full possibilities the problem must be examined in some detail. In general we must distinguish four different problems connected with the health of the child below school age. First, there is the problem of maternal mortality. This can justly be classified as a child-health problem because the health of the child depends so absolutely on the mother's health. Secondly, there is the problem of infant hygiene during the first month of life. The health of the child from the second to the twelfth months inclusive forms a third problem; for the two different periods of the first year are quite separate from the point of view of health. The principal causes of death in the first month are generally not the same as the causes operating during the months which follow. Finally, we have the question of the health of the *pre-school child,* using this term in its technical sense to include the child between his first and his sixth birthday.

The problem of maternal mortality is a very pressing one. It is a very regrettable fact that our rate is higher than that of any civilized country. To find the causes of this state of affairs it is necessary to examine the data in some detail. Frankel (5) studied the rates of maternal death from various causes during the period of 1917 to 1924 in 17 states. The 1924 rates in these states are shown in Table I. It will be seen that the outstanding cause of death is puerperal sepsis and strangely enough this is a factor which could be almost entirely eliminated with the adoption of appropriate measures; for its mode of transmission has been fairly well understood since the work of Semmelweiss in 1847. A great deal of progress has been made, it is true. Thirty or forty years ago the death rate from this cause was over 400. But the surprising thing is not that the rate has been reduced but that the reduction has not been greater. Frankel finds that in the period from 1917 to 1924 the trend of the mortality showed a decrease of only 1.4 per cent per year, which compares unfavorably with what public-health work has accomplished with other controllable diseases. For during the same period the tuberculosis and diphtheria death rates have declined about four per cent a year while typhoid has declined about eight per cent per year. It might reasonably be expected that sepsis would show a similar decline.

Perhaps Levy's (7) study explains why this has not happened. This investigator studied the maternal mortality rate in Newark for the period 1916 to 1921. On cases handled by a midwife the maternal mortality was 1.5 per thousand births as compared with the general death rate of 4.3. Possibly the crowded condition of the curriculum of our medical schools does not allow sufficient time for the instruction of students in this important subject. It has been suggested too that physicians have a tendency to hasten delivery by instrumental means where the midwife more wisely allows Nature to take its course.

## TABLE I

Causes of Maternal Mortality in Seven States and the District of Columbia in 1924 according to Frankel. (Maternal Deaths, per 100,000 live births).

| | |
|---|---|
| Puerperal Sepsis | 241 |
| Eclampsia | 165 |
| Accidents of Labor | 64 |
| Accidents of Pregnancy | 58 |
| Other causes | 102 |
| Total | 630 |

The second cause of maternal mortality, eclampsia, shows a slightly more favorable decline during the period covered by Frankel's study (5) ; namely, 1.7 per cent per year. However, there is no reason why, with proper supervision during pregnancy, it could not be reduced much more. The figures for accidents of labor and for accidents of pregnancy are disturbed by the abnormal rate during the influenza epidemic of 1918-1920. It is probable that if the effects of the epidemic were eliminated these two causes would show no definite trend in either direction. It would probably be possible to reduce them, however, by proper supervision of the mother during pregnancy.

A great deal can be done by good legislation toward solving the problem of infant mortality. The practice of midwifery should be regulated. Every state except Massachusetts has some legislation affecting midwives (13). The best practice requires a woman to hold a license before she may act in this capacity. This makes it possible to demand certain standards before a license is granted.

The welfare of the working mother must be safeguarded. Woodbury (18) found an enormously higher infant mortality rate among the children of mothers employed either during pregnancy or shortly before the birth of the child than among other children. He found too that this could not be accounted for by racial or social factors. Five states have at the present time laws prohibiting the employment of mothers for specified periods before and after confinement, while a sixth state, Washington, secures the same results by an order of its Industrial Welfare Commission having the force of law. These laws, however, are poorly enforced and there seems to be little tendency to enact further legislation of this sort.

The control of venereal disease is a child-welfare problem of great importance. In recent years there has been a general movement to deal more severely with prostitution by legal means. Even more important are the efforts being made to cope with this problem through educational and public-health measures.

Still another piece of progressive legislation is the compulsory reportability of the puerperal sepsis which is required in 18 states (11). Again, legislation giving the state certain supervision of hospitals and maternity homes has been found by experience to be a useful measure.

The maternity center is a comparatively new agency but it has already accomplished a great deal. Such a center needs at least three rooms, a waiting room, an examining room for the doctor, and a dressing room for the patients. In such centers the physician may hold consultations at least twice a week, while a nurse should be on duty there during certain hours every day. The center generally makes an effort to get in touch with every expectant mother not under the care of a private physician. The records should give all available information concerning the woman's health. Expectant mothers should visit the center once a month during pregnancy and oftener as the time of confinement approaches. Besides this, the nurse should visit them at home every week or two. Regular urinalyses should be made and the mother should be instructed to call the nurse at once if any abnormal condition should develop. The nurse helps her prepare a layette and the center makes sure that arrangements have been made for the woman's confinement either at a hospital or under the care of her private physician or a midwife (2).

If the establishment of a maternity center is not possible a great deal may be accomplished through the work of visiting or district nurses. Frequently community physicians will coöperate with such nurses to hold consultations. Where the services of a physician are not available the nurse does about the same type of work as is done by a nurse connected with a maternity center, but since no center is available for examination the woman must be referred to her own private physician, or to a clinic.

Although considerable progress has been made in the organization of maternity clinics and in the field of public health a great deal more remains to be done. The American Child Health Association survey (1) shows an average in the 86 cities studied of 39 visits to maternity centers per thousand births, which compares unfavorably with the Appraisal Form standards of 250 visits. Again, the same study gives 458 as the average number of visits made by public-health nurses in this connection while the standards require one thousand. Maternity hygiene is characterized by a startling unevenness. There were cities in which no work at all was being done and there were other cities in which the standards were more than doubled. Let us hope that during the next few years the same high standards will prevail throughout the whole country which have been reached by some cities.

A great deal also might be accomplished by closer supervision of obstetrics. It is questioned by many whether the present tendency to hospitalize all maternity cases is a wise procedure. The answer probably is that women are generally best confined in hospitals, but only in hospitals which maintain high standards of obstetrical work. This implies a preliminary examination of admissions to the maternity ward, and their complete segregation from other types of patients during their entire stay in the hospital, together with a rigidly aseptic technique at all times.

A minor problem in this connection, and yet a problem of considerable importance, is the prevention of *ophthalmia neonatorum* (4). In 1907-1908, 26.6 per cent of the children admitted to schools for the blind had lost their vision from birth infections. The pathetic thing about this fact is that these eye infections are entirely preventable by a very simple measure; namely, the treatment of the child's eyes immediately after birth with silver nitrate or similar prophylactic solution. The use of such a solution is now quite generally required by state laws and ophthalmia itself is reportable in all states and territories except Alaska.

It has already been stated that over one-half of the infants who die under one year of age meet death in the first month. Public-health work has been able to accomplish very little in reducing the death rate during this period. It may seem strange that while the problem of mortality between the first and twelfth month has yielded to modern methods, relatively little has been accomplished in the first month. The reasons for this condition are investigated by Frankel (5). He made a detailed analysis of the infant death rate for the states which he was studying. He found that between 1917 and 1925 the death rate for prematurity has been declining at the rate of 0.8 per cent per year. In the same period the rate for congenital malformations has shown an average decrease each year of 0.6 per cent. Syphilis has shown a marked decline, amounting to 6.1 per cent per year, if the figures are reliable, a thing which Frankel doubts. But by all odds the most interesting thing shown by his study is the fact that the death rate from injuries at birth has *increased* 5.3 per cent annually. Woodbury confirms this last statement. His study (19) shows that deaths from injury at birth increased 23 per cent in the United States Birth Registration Area between 1915 and 1921.

There seem to be no reasons why these rates cannot be reduced still more. Williams of Hopkins has shown in a carefully controlled experiment that it is possible to reduce the proportion of deaths in the two weeks of life of the babies of syphilitic mothers from 52 to 7 per cent, the former figure representing the rate for the babies of those who did not and the second of those who did receive antisyphilitic treatment. Prematurity and congenital malformations can be controlled by bettering the general hygiene of the expectant mother. But the most hopeful point of attack is the death rate from injuries at birth. There is no earthly reason why this should increase. It would probably be possible to reduce it materially by better obstetrical practice.

There is also considerable hope for improvement in the hygiene of the group of infants between one and twelve months of age. It has been said already that this is the period in which our most outstanding work has been accomplished. According to Frankel's figures covering the years 1918 to 1925 the death rate in the first year of life for diarrhea and enteritis has been decreasing 9.38 per cent per year. Measles has shown a decline of 3.93 per cent, whooping cough, 6.24 per cent, tuberculosis, 9.63 per cent, and diphtheria, 5.89 per cent annually. The acute respiratory diseases have also shown a sharp decline but the trend is not significant on account of the abnormal conditions during the influenza years.

The reduction of the infant mortality rate for

the period in question may be hastened by encouraging breast feeding. Woodbury (18) reports that infant mortality rate among artificially fed children averaged three or four times as great as that among the breast fed. The difference was especially marked for gastric and intestinal diseases, the rate being 7.7 times as high among the artificially fed as among the other group. Where breast feeding is not possible scientific formula feeding is a good substitute. The dissemination of information on this point is an important public-health measure. The secret of success is to educate parents in the essentials of child care and to keep them in touch with the physician for advice when special difficulties arise. The child-health center and the public-health nurse have been the two chief means of bringing this about.

The child-health center has a comparatively long history, for it goes back at least to the year 1890, when Professor Herrgott founded *L'Oeuvre de la Maternité* at Nancy. The first station of this sort in the United States was opened by Nathan Straus in New York City in 1893. These stations may be classified into three types. One type distributes modified milk in sanitary feeding bottles, the second type provides instruction for the mother and health supervision for the baby, while the third type includes both sorts of service.

Baby-health stations of the third type are the most common and hopeful answer to the problem of the infant death rate. The best of such stations have at least three rooms. One of these is used as a waiting room for dispensing milk, in the second the babies are undressed and weighed, while the third is for the use of the doctor. The center should be opened at regular hours and the nurse should always be available to give advice while the doctor, himself, should hold regular consultations once or twice a week. Besides this, the nurse should make regular visits to the home of all mothers for the purpose of giving supervision and direction in regard to the baby's environment in the home. The type of work done in these stations has an enormous effect on the infant death rate. Mayer found in his study of the baby-health stations of New York that the death rates among infants receiving attention at them was less than one-half the general rate of New York City. Similar results have often been observed in the course of the administration of the Federal Maternity and Infancy Act. For example, the 677 white and 996 colored babies whose mothers had received prenatal care at the Louisville City Hospital showed infant mortality rates of 23.6 and 39.2 respectively, which compares favorably with the corresponding general rates in that city of 38.2 and 55.1 (16, page 66). Considering the remarkable effect of this work the cost is very small. It varies from 60 cents to $1.50 per month per baby. The baby-health station and the maternity center are often combined into one station.

The value of the child-health center is very greatly increased when it is combined with a good system of public-health nursing. It is thus possible to reach the child who is too sick to be brought to the clinic and the mother who is not sufficiently interested to come of her own accord. It is possible for the nurse to give advice more intelligently when she has seen the child's home and gained some knowledge of the problems existing there. This work has progressed rapidly, since the first laws were passed in Massachusetts and Pennsylvania in 1911 authorizing the employment of public-health nurses. At the present time the American Child Health Association finds an average of 2,345 visits by public health nurses per thousand children under two years of age, a figure which compares not badly with the standard of 2,500 (1).

The problem of the pre-school child has not been met to the same extent as the problem of

infant health. No social agency has really been
developed to meet the problem. There are, however, two or three tendencies. One is to reach
these children through the baby-health stations.
Since these have been so successful with infants
under one year of age there seems to be no good
reason why they should not do equally good
work with children until they are old enough to
go to school.

Another agency is the day nursery, the history
of which in the United States goes back at least
to 1854 with the foundation of the day nursery
in connection with the Nursery and Children's
Hospital of New York City. There are now several hundred of these institutions in the United
States. The nursery requires several rooms.
There should be at least the following: a playroom for children between two and six years of
age, a nursery with cribs for the younger children, a dining room, a cloakroom, an isolation-
room, lavatories, and bathrooms. The nursery
must be in charge of competent and trained people. Under their guidance such institutions can
make a definite contribution to the health of the
young child. This can be done first by watching
the children closely for the first signs of contagious disease, isolating them immediately, and
giving them appropriate treatment. It can be

done also by the detection and correction of physical defects and by assuring the children proper nutrition and a hygienic daily routine.

The day nursery, however, is open to the objection that it takes the child away from its home. It is a fundamental principle of modern social work that the best place for the young child is its own home. The day nursery therefore finds many opponents who declare that no mother with young children should be forced to go to work. If necessary, the community should make her financially able to care for her child at home through mothers' pensions.

It has been frequently remarked that the day nursery is rapidly losing ground. Lewinski-Corwin (8) studied the day nurseries of New York City and found that they were being used only to three-fourths of their capacity. He found also that only one-fourth of them were "conscious of the health aspect of their work." It seems therefore as if child-health work cannot expect very much of the day nursery.

A more recent movement is the nursery school, generally admitting children between the ages of two and five. The child may spend a shorter day at this type of institution than at the day nursery. The object is not to relieve the mother of the responsibility of caring for her child but rather to afford her expert advice and to give the child its first social contact with other children of its own age in a controlled environment. Whether the nursery school will ever become universal is a question, but certainly this type of institution is doing a very valuable work through its research activities.

Besides these specific measures which have been urged in the present chapter to meet particular problems, there are certain general educational measures which serve to give a more intelligent attack on the problem as a whole. Such are the special public campaigns of which by far the most famous was the *Children's Year*, conducted under the auspices of the Children's Bureau beginning April 6, 1918. Such also are the *Baby Health Weeks* which are held frequently by local groups in various places. Progressive health departments and parent-teacher groups are doing a great deal by the use of study clubs, lectures, libraries, and movies to spread the knowledge of the fundamental principles of child hygiene among the people.

By all odds the most important educational work at present carried on in the field of maternal and infant hygiene is that sponsored by the United States Children's Bureau and coöperating states under the provisions of the Maternity and Infancy Act of 1921. Although this work has taken different forms in various states it has uniformly been educational in character. Sometimes this educational work has taken the form of instruction to individuals through permanent or itinerant conferences or home visits. Sometimes the appeal has been directed to groups rather than individuals through lectures, motion pictures, and exhibits. Again literature on maternal or infant hygiene has been distributed. Although it is not possible to measure directly the effect of this work there can be little doubt that it has played a most important part in the recent reduction of infant mortality.

One of the most hopeful attacks on the whole problem of maternal and child hygiene is the new movement for parenthood education. By this term is understood the education of children for parenthood. Vocational education is now a recognized feature of our school system. We have given children systematic preparation for many trades and occupations, but it is only very recently that we have given them any training in the most common vocation of all—the job of being a parent. Such instruction, however, is certainly in keeping with the newer spirit in public-health work which seeks to forestall unhygienic conditions through education. It is certainly logical enough to reach the future mother at the earliest moment, while she is a girl in school.

Although this type of instruction has been tried out in various places, Wisconsin has been the first state to introduce a course in infant hygiene into the schools as part of the state course of study. The Wisconsin course may therefore be taken as typical of the present tendencies. In the fall of 1924 ten one-hour lessons in infant hygiene were worked out and made a part of the course of study of that state. These lessons were mandatory only for the vocational high school but according to Whitcomb (17) they have been quite generally adopted in the larger cities and are becoming increasingly popular in the rural districts. The course is usually made part of the home economics instruction in the city schools, while the rural schools generally make it part of the physiology and hygiene work of the eighth grade. It is recommended that the course in infant hygiene be demonstrated and a standard equipment has been designed for this purpose. Girls who complete the course satisfactorily receive a semiformal diploma.

An example of a more elaborate program is furnished by the work done in the Highland Park High School, Highland Park, Michigan.

This institution maintains a nursery school and offers to its pupils a one-semester course of three 45-minute periods per week in child care and parenthood education. One of these periods is devoted to classroom work, while the other two periods are spent in observation and duties in connection with the nursery school. Besides this, the students spend in the nursery school one entire day each month. This combination of class work with the actual child care would seem to be a very hopeful tendency in education for parenthood.

Colleges and universities are naturally able to offer more advanced courses in child care. Some of these are designed for students who intend to become teachers in nursery schools; others are for those who wish thus to prepare themselves for parenthood. The best of these courses are organized in connection with a nursery school. For example, Ohio State University offers a course in child, and parenthood education to all students who have fulfilled the prerequisites. It consists of four one-hour lectures and four two-hour laboratory periods per week for 12 weeks. The laboratory work is done at the University's nursery school which was opened in February, 1925. Other institutions which offer similar courses and which do not maintain nursery schools, sometimes supplement their theoretical instruction with observation work in clinics, or in the homes of young children.

The future of child-health work appears bright. Probably great advances will be made in the next decades. There are particularly three recent developments of great significance. The first is the increase in the number of workers at present doing research in child development. The National Research Council was able to list 425 such investigators in March, 1927, (9). With this increased knowledge of childhood we shall be able to plan for child-health more intelligently. The second development is the growth of the new profession of scientific child care. In our university courses and nursery schools, numbers of young women are preparing to take up the profession of child care as a life work. The third dvelopment is the tendency to standardize our child-health work, which has been somewhat sporadic and uneven in the past—a tendency which makes itself felt partly through state supervision and partly through the voluntary adoption of standards. All these new developments bear rich promise for the future.

## BIBLIOGRAPHY

(1) American Child Health Association, Research Division: *A health survey of* 86 *cities*. New York, American Child Health Association, 1925. xxxiv, 614 p.
Reports a survey of all American cities whose population was between 40,000 and 70,000 in 1920.

(2) Baker, Sara Josephine: *Child hygiene*. New York and London, Harper & Brothers, 1925. xii, 534 p.
Perhaps the best reference on the subject.

(3) Collins, Selwyn D.: "Infant mortality from different causes and at different ages in nine cities of the United States." *Pub. Health Rep.*, 43:392-403, February 17, 1928.
Unexpected differences exist between the different cities.

(4) Conference of State and Provincial Health Authorities of North America—Standing Committee on Conservation of Vision: *Prevention of blindness in new-born babies*. New York, The National Committee for the Prevention of Blindness. Reprint from the *Proceedings of the Forty-first Annual Meeting of the Conference of State and Provincial Health Authorities of North America*. May, 1926. pp. 92-117.
The prevention of *ophthalmia neonatorum*.

(5) Frankel, Lee K.: *The present status of maternal and infant hygiene in the United States*. New York, Metropolitan Life Insurance Company, 1927. 30 p.
An excellent review and analysis.

(6) Green, Howard Whipple: "An analysis of infant mortality by causes." *Jr. of Preventive Medicine.* 1:391-400, May, 1927.

"Infant mortality has been greatly reduced during the past generation. . . . The decrease in the number of deaths due to diarrhea and enteritis is largely responsible for this reduction."

(7) Levy, Julius: "Maternal mortality and mortality in the first month of life in relation to attendant at birth." *Am. Jr. of Public Health,* 13:88-95, February, 1923.

Mothers attended by midwives and their children both did unexpectedly well.

(8) Lewinski-Corwin, E. H.: *Day nurseries in New York City; a summary of the principal findings of the study made by the Public Health Committee of the New York Academy of Medicine.* New York, Association of Day Nurseries of New York City, 1924. Pages not numbered.

Summary of a study.

(9) Marston, Leslie Ray: *Directory of research in child development.* Washington, National Research Council, 1927. 38 p. (Reprint and Circular Series of the National Research Council. No. 76.)

Lists all research projects known to this agency.

(10) Metropolitan Life Insurance Co.: "A historical retrospect on expectation of life." *Statistical Bulletin of the Metropolitan Life Insurance Company,* 8(11):1-4, November, 1927 and 9 (3):5-11, March, 1928.

Treats of the increase of length of life in recent years.

(11) Mosher, George Clark: *The problem of compulsory notification of puerperal septicemia.* Washington, D. C., U. S. Gov't Printing Office, 1927. 13 p. (Separate No. 1 from Children's Bureau Publication No. 181.)

Analyzes state legislation.

(12) Pirquet, C.: "The decrease of the death rate except among the new-born." *Monthly Epidemiological Reports of the Health Section of the League of Nations.* 5:584-95, September 15, 1926.
In England and Wales the decrease has been mainly for ages over one month.

(13) Rude, Anna E.: "The midwife problem in the United States." *Jr. American Med. Assn.,* 81:987-92, September 22, 1923.

(14) Rude, Anna E.: *Physical status of pre-school children; Gary, Ind.* Washington, D. C., U. S. Gov't Printing Office, 1922. 84 p. (Children's Bureau Publication No. 111.)

(15) U. S. Bureau of the Census: *Birth, stillbirth, and infant mortality statistics for the Birth Registration Area of the United States,* 1924. Washington, D. C., U. S. Gov't Printing Office, 1926. 283 p.
The official source of these statistics.

(16) U. S. Children's Bureau: *The promotion of the welfare and hygiene of maternity and infancy; the administration of the Act of Congress of November 23, 1921, for the fiscal year ended June 30, 1927.* Washington, D. C., U. S. Gov't Printing Office, 1928. vi, 150 p. (Children's Bureau Publication No. 186).
The results of the administration of the Federal Maternity and Infancy Acts.

(17) Whitcomb, Emeline S.: *Typical child care and parenthood education in home economics departments.* Washington, D. C., U. S. Gov't Printing Office, 1927. v, 62 p. (Bureau of Education Bulletin, 1927, No. 17.)
Covers the courses in these subjects in grammar and secondary schools and in institutions for higher education.

(18) Woodbury, Robert Morse: *Causal factors in infant mortality; a statistical study based on investigations in eight cities.* Washington, D. C., U. S. Gov't Printing Office, 1925. xi, 245 p. (Children's Bureau Publication No. 142.)
A statistical investigation of infant mortality.

(19) Woodbury, Robert Morse: "Decline in infant mortality in the United States Birth Registration Area 1915-21." *Am. Jr. Public Health*, 13:377-83, May, 1923.
An analysis of the trends in six years.

# CHAPTER III

## *Child Health—The School Child*

The newer view of the school's function is strikingly exemplified in its health work. A generation or two ago the school was expected to train the child's mind and to do nothing else. To-day it is expected to prepare its pupils for complete living and this implies an interest in the child's health as well as in his mental development.

The school's first responsibility in the matter of child health obviously is that the pupils should not be injured by their school experience. The crowding together of many children from different environments in a more or less intimate physical contact naturally makes possible the rapid spread of contagious diseases. The long periods of sedentary occupations are unnatural for growing boys and girls. School health work must begin by combating such evils.

Modern educators, however, are not satisfied with this minimum. They realize that the school

54

must not only not injure the child but that it must help him by constructive measures to become and remain healthy. As a consequence of this principle the present century has seen the rapid growth of medical supervision and health education.

It was said above that the school's first responsibility is to provide healthful surroundings for the pupil so that his attendance at school may not injure him. In spite of the obvious nature of this principle there is very much room for improvement in the physical conditions of our school buildings. Only about one-half of the states have regulations with regard to the provision of drinking fountains. More than one-fourth of the state laws do not provide for the supply of toilets. About one-half of the states have no specific laws on school ventilation (18).

It may thus be seen that legislation regarding the sanitation of school buildings leaves a good deal to be desired. Moreover, it is unfortunately true that even the existing state legislation is not always carefully followed in practice. Many of our rural districts show an appalling lack of provision for the most elementary sanitary conditions in the schools. Even our cities fall far short of perfection in this regard. A survey (1) made by the American Child Health Associa-

tion and covering 86 cities with populations between forty and seventy thousand, found that
eight of these cities still had the common drinking cup in one or more of their schools, while
27 still had at least some outside toilets. In only
37 of the cities were all the schools properly
protected against fire hazards. Common pencils
were found in half the cities. In many school
systems the cleanliness of the classrooms and
particularly of the toilets left a great deal to be
desired.

In recent years there has been a movement to
provide so-called "health schools" for malnourished or tubercular children. It has been well
said that the term itself implies a consciousness
that our present schools are not as healthy as
they might be. If the ordinary classroom is not
a proper place for the child in delicate health,
is it a proper place for the normal child?

Many have argued that the average school
and the average curriculum do considerable
damage to the pupil. A number of early studies
on this point are summarized by Terman (19).
Although some of these investigations may be
criticized from the standpoint of strict scientific
method there is undoubtedly a general correla-
tion between school attendance and ill health.
The routine of modern education often imposes

a severe strain on the physique of the child and the result is a nervous, tired, and weakened child at the end of the school year.

The site of the modern school building should be selected with a view to hygiene as well as to other requirements. While it is naturally difficult to secure ideal surroundings in the most crowded sections of the city, whenever it is possible the buildings should be situated on a plot of ground large enough to assure plenty of play space, fresh air, and sunlight. The buildings should be so oriented that there will be sufficient light in each classroom with a minimum of glare. Naturally there must be adequate provisions for safety in case of fire. Drinking fountains, lavatories, and toilet facilities should be of the most modern and sanitary type.

Great care must be exercised in planning the classroom, for herein the children spend a considerable proportion of their waking time. The best modern practice limits the length of the room to about 32 feet. The width should not be more than twice the height of the top of the windows from the floor and the window space should be at least equal to one-fifth of the floor space. The height of the room should be about 12½ or 13 feet. In order to impose a minimum of strain on the child's eyes the walls should be painted or tinted in a soft shade of brown or green and the paint should be without gloss. Blackboards should not be placed by the windows nor be subject to cross light. They should be washed thoroughly every day so as to provide a dull black surface for writing.

Seats and desks which are adjustable in accordance with the child's size are now fairly common in our schools. There is no magic in such furniture, however, and it is no better than the old-fashioned unadjustable type unless the adjustable feature is used and every seat and desk is fitted to its occupant.

It will be much easier to prevent the spread of disease if there are facilities for keeping clothing either in individual lockers or in cloakrooms which are large enough so that the clothing of one child will not come into contact with that of another. For the same reason modern standards require the use of individual drinking cups and towels. Also, each child ought to have his own pencil.

Probably there is no more mooted question in connection with school sanitation than the ventilation question. The difference of opinion is between the advocates of mechanical ventilation systems and the advocates of open-window ventilation. Until rather recently it was generally agreed that mechanical systems were superior and they were required by the laws of about half the states (22). But recent studies, particularly that of the New York Commission on Ventilation, have thrown considerable doubt on the superiority of mechanical systems. Good ventilation is possible under either system; but the open-window system is probably cheaper to install and to operate and less likely to get out of order. The New York Commission therefore concludes "that window ventilation with ample direct radiation, window deflectors and adequate gravity exhaust, seems the most generally promising method for the ventilation of the classroom" (15). More important than the type of system is its intelligent use. No type will give satisfactory results unless the janitor and the teachers coöperate to keep the air of the classroom at a temperature of about 66 to 68 degrees and to provide for frequent changes of air without draughts (22, 24).

The problem of school hygiene becomes particularly acute in times of epidemic. Children crowded together in a classroom offer a ready medium for the spread of contagious disease. It has been the practice in the past to close all schools under such circumstances. A survey conducted by the Bureau of Education seems to show that such closure of schools "is an extremely clumsy, unscientific, and unsatisfactory method of controlling epidemics among school children. It results not only in loss of school time and money, but it fails to control, inasmuch as infected children are at large, playing in the street, without restriction, and therefore spreading the infection" (fide 3).

Closing the schools is a measure which may be justified in some special cases, for instance, when an epidemic is entirely out of control, when the cause of the disease is unknown, or when there is no adequate health supervision in the schools. In other cases, however, it is felt that better results may be obtained if the child be required to attend school and an intensive effort made to meet the problem there. This would imply the frequent examination of all children by the school physician and nurses as well as by the classroom teacher, with the isolation and treatment of each case as it is discovered. Under such circumstances recess is held at different times for each grade, group games are discouraged, the children are told to come directly to school in the morning and to go directly home at night, and places where children gather out of school (as movie theaters) should be closed to children. By these various measures the associa-

tion of the children with each other is mini-
mized. Under this system, although there is a
certain amount of contact among the children
in school it is felt that this is little more than the
contact which would result from their play. On
the other hand, keeping the children in school
provides them with an intensive health supervision which they would lack if the schools were
closed.

The attention of the public is focused sharply
on the school in times of epidemics and measures to prevent contagion are watched with interest. But in the long run the work of the school
in preventing the spread of contagious diseases
in ordinary times is probably more important
than the emergency measures adopted when epidemics are raging. Under the latter conditions
a few children may fall victims to the disease
but their number is probably smaller than the
number of those who succumb to diseases caught
in the classroom under ordinary conditions.

To prevent this latter form of contagion pupils must be carefully watched for the first signs
of communicable disease. The American Child
Health Association in their survey (1) spoken
of above found that in 33 out of the 86 cities
studied the children were inspected daily for
signs of infectious disease. In ten others this

was done weekly. The duty generally falls to the teacher or the school nurse. In 11 communities it fell to the former and in 21 to the latter, while in 18 cities the nurse and teacher divided the responsibility between them. Inspection by a physician was much less common. In simple justice to the child, inspection should be made a daily routine. It should be in the first instance the duty of the teacher to carry it out and she should receive some training for this in normal school. When she finds a case which arouses her suspicion the school nurse or the school physician should be summoned.

Another measure of great importance in the control of contagious disease is the immunization of all children against smallpox and diphtheria. The former is now a fairly common practice. The American Child Health Association survey found that smallpox vaccination was compulsory in more than one-half of the cities studied. This measure, however, was not always efficiently enforced. For even in the cities where vaccination was required an average of only 87 per cent of the fifth grade children were actually found vaccinated. Toxin-antitoxin immunization against diphtheria is newer and therefore not so usual. The above survey showed, however, that 40 of the 86 cities had at least made a start in this work. At the present time a beginning is being made with the Dick innoculation against scarlet fever in some school systems. There seems to be no valid reason why all these measures should not become universal. It would evidently be a great victory in the cause of child health if they became routine practices in all our schools.

Most of the measures thus far reviewed have as their object to prevent the child from being harmed physically by his school experience. Modern education, however, has advanced beyond this stage and now aims not only to prevent the spread of contagious diseases but also to teach positive health. The necessity for this changed attitude is evident from the great prevalence of remediable physical defects in our school population. The results of school medical examinations bear witness to the fact that the majority of the children suffer from some physical defect needing correction. The pathetic thing about the situation is that if no one takes the slight trouble to correct these defects in childhood they will become more serious with the lapse of years until the adult finds himself grievously handicapped by serious physical ailments.

Wood (quoted in 3) has estimated that three-fourths of our school children have physical defects calling for treatment. It would certainly seem to be a conservative statement to say that two-thirds belong in this class. Of these children some show more than a single condition calling for medical care so that it has been the experience of school physicians that there are generally to be found at least one thousand defects per one thousand of the school population. For example, results of compulsory medical examination in New York State (excluding New York City, Rochester, and Buffalo and excluding also private and parochial schools) show that 595,206 children examined in the school year of 1923-1924 had 605,028 physical defects (12).

Unfortunately the results of school medical examinations will not often bear very much analysis. They are usually made very hurriedly and sometimes by persons without proper medical training. Newmayer (14), studying the results of physical examinations by 70 physicians, found that one physician had discovered anaemia in .5 per cent and another in 25.0 per cent of the children examined. It is hardly credible that there were only one-fiftieth as many anaemic children in the group examined by the former as in the group examined by the

latter; and we can only conclude that the examining doctors were using very different standards. The same conclusion must be made when
the same author reports defective vision in 1.5
per cent and 24.0 per cent respectively, according to different physicians, and defective tonsils
in 2 to 35 per cent. These discrepancies exist not
merely between the reports of different individual physicians but between the reports of
different cities as well. Thus the United States
Public Health Service survey (20) reports that
two cities found eye defects in 20 to 30 per cent
of their school population, while 32 cities found
them in one to five per cent.

Perhaps the commonest of all defects reported
is carious teeth. Wood estimated that over 50
per cent of the children have this condition. The
New York State figures quoted above and representing the largest single group of examinations at present available to the writer report
this condition present in 36.0 per cent of the
children. Newmayer (14) estimates that the figure should be about 35 per cent. These reports
and estimates, however, were usually based upon
hurried examinations made without mirror and
probe. Where a dentist or dental hygienist makes
the examination the figures are very much
higher. Thus a survey made by the New York

Association for Improving the Condition of the Poor and including 2,186 children from 2 to 18 years of age found that 96 per cent had carious teeth. The Division of Dental Hygiene of Bridgeport (5) reports that "In schools or districts where little or no attention has been given to mouth hygiene it is difficult to find three children out of one hundred entirely free from dental defects." On the whole Rogers (18) is probably conservative when he states that 90 to 95 per cent of the entire school population suffer from carious teeth.

Even more important, although less widespread, are defects of vision. Here again figures vary widely. Wood sets the figure at 25 per cent. The New York State returns give 8.5 per cent. Newmayer estimated that the figure should be about 12 per cent, while Terman (19) quotes a number of older reports averaging between 20 and 30 per cent. Probably the most reliable results are given by the Eye Sight Conservation survey (9), including more than eight hundred thousand children from various cities. From these results it appears that about 22 per cent of children are suffering from defects of vision and out of this 22 per cent 9 per cent have had their defects corrected by glasses and 13 per cent have not.

An even wider diversity exists on the question of defects of hearing. Terman quotes results which set the proportion of children with ear defects anywhere from 0.5 per cent to 50 per cent. The New York State survey reported diseased or defective ears in 1.3 per cent of the children. Fortunately there now exists a truly objective technique for measuring defects of hearing. This is the Seashore audiometer. In this device the child is supplied with a phonographic attachment which he applies to the ear to be tested while four columns of figures are dictated one at a time with decreasing intensity of sound. The child writes down the numbers as they are dictated and the number of figures written down correctly is an index of his acuity of hearing. The Commission of Education of the American Federation of Organizations for the Hard of Hearing (2) reports results of audiometer tests. A hearing loss of nine "sensation units" was taken as a criterion of deafness. A person showing this degree of deafness would have to come within two-fifths of the average hearing distance of the normal person before he could hear. Using this liberal standard the commission found that in a group of 4112 pupils tested 14.4 per cent were defective in at least one ear and that out of these 3.2 per cent were defective in both ears. It has been found, moreover, that the children defective in one ear are quite severely handicapped.

Another common condition revealed by examinations consists of naso-pharyngeal defects. Wood estimated that 30 per cent of the children have enlarged tonsils or cervical glands or adenoids which need attention. The New York State figures show tonsilar conditions needing treatment in 19.6 per cent of children and defective nasal breathing in another 5.4 per cent.

Malnutrition is a condition whose prevalence it is rather difficult to estimate. Wood believed that about one-fourth of the school pupils deserved to be classified as malnourished. In an effort to diagnose this condition the use of height-weight tables has become popular. These give a standard weight for every height and age. Children falling below these standards by a certain per cent are classified as undernourished. The most widely used of thse standards are the Baldwin-Wood tables. It was commonly assumed that a child ten per cent under these standards was a malnourished child.

More recent studies have shown that this criterion is very unreliable. Clark (6) found that of the children who were ten per cent or more underweight according to the United States

Public Health Service norms only 38.2 per cent were classified as malnourished by these expert physicians. Similar conclusions were reached by Dublin and Gebhart (8) in connection with the Wood tables. It is felt now that on account of sharp differences in physical type no mere weight standard is accurate enough to serve for the diagnosis of malnutrition.

This diagnosis must be made by a trained physician and for his guidance some such standard as the Dunfermline Scale is useful. Baker and Blumenthal (4) found in a study of New York children that about one-fourth were undernourished judged by this most scientific of standards. It would seem, therefore, that the problem of bad nourishment is a serious one for the school child. Roberts (16) gives an excellent popular exposition of this subject.

Besides these more common physical defects a certain per cent of the children examined always show more serious conditions. Thus Wood estimates that about one and one-half to two per cent of our school pupils have organic heart disease, about five per cent have or have had tuberculosis, while another five per cent have serious orthopedic defects.

The school's duty in regard to the physical defects of pupils is clear enough in general outline.  The defects should be discovered through careful, periodic physical examinations and then they should be remedied.

Physical examinations of some sort are authorized in at least 42 states, while in some of the remaining states such examinations are carried on under the control of local authorities (7, 18). This legislation, however, leaves much to be desired. For in some cases the law is merely permissive, while in others it does not apply to all children. In only 16 states is the law mandatory for all pupils in all districts.

Even where the law applies to all children it is often carried out in an inefficient manner. The American Child Health Association survey found medical inspection of some sort in 82 out of 86 cities studied. About three-fifths of these cities try to examine children annually but only 23 make this annual examination apply to all the children. Again, the physicians do not allow enough time to go over each child carefully. Out of 62 cities where data on this point were gathered, in 35 the physicians spent less than two minutes on each child and in only five did they spend more than ten minutes. The average time was less than three and one-half minutes. Out of 65 cities in only nine were the children stripped to the waist as a routine procedure.

This was done occasionally in six more. In 24 the clothing was not even loosened at the neck. In at least 16 cities the examination took place in the classroom. Besides this, school physicians are notoriously ill paid. According to Rogers (18) the remuneration varies from 42 cents to 4 dollars an hour. The physical examination in the school, therefore, is only too likely to be a procedure in which an untrained person or physician of inferior ability glances hurriedly for a minute or two at a child amid distracting surroundings and without the possibility of having the child remove enough clothing to make an examination of the heart and lungs worth while.

It seems a truth too evident to be insisted upon that the discovery of defects without their treatment is quite useless. However, this has been very frequently the case in our schools. Even in excellent school systems such as New York or Philadelphia only about one-half the defects are corrected. The American Child Health Association survey reports that in the average city studied, so far as data were available, only about 30 per cent of the eye defects, 43 per cent of the dental defects, and 14 per cent of the nasopharyngeal defects were treated. In contrast to this in a Philadelphia normal school 96.3 per cent, and in the Connecticut State normal schools almost 100 per cent of corrections were reported. The reason for these latter high figures was that the student teachers were required to have their defects corrected if they wished to remain students of the schools. Many feel that one day we shall take a similar attitude with respect to the child in the grammar grades. If vaccination may be required by law there seems no reason why the correction of defects should not be equally insisted upon.

It would seem that a satisfactory health supervision program should include the following elements: It should be in charge of a full-time physician. Moreover, the salary of this official ought to be high enough to attract a thoroughly competent man. In making the routine school examination he may be assisted by part-time physicians. These men should examine all children every year. Each child should be allowed at least ten minutes for the examination. His parents and teacher should be present in order that they may appreciate the child's condition and discuss it at once with the physician. The examination should take place in a quiet room other than the classroom and the clothing should be partially removed. Besides these thorough examinations the classroom teacher and the school nurse should make frequent cursory inspections to detect the beginning of communicable diseases.

The follow-up work will be largely the responsibility of the school nurse. She should visit the child's home, explain to his parents the importance of having the physical defects remedied, and should advise them to take the child to their own physician. Where this is impossible for financial reasons the nurse should arrange an appointment for the child at a clinic. It is generally agreed that there must be a nurse to every two thousand children if this work is to be done efficiently—a standard which is seldom found in practice. The United States Health Service survey reports (20) in 98 out of the 100 largest cities in the country there was an average of but 3.16 school nurses per ten thousand children.

Certain cases will not yield to this simple procedure. For example, children with incipient tuberculosis need a long treatment, including special food, open air, sunlight, and carefully supervised exercise. The school nurse will find that little can be done in such cases if the children are kept in the ordinary classroom. For this reason there has arisen a movement for special open-air schools, first established in the United States in Providence in 1908. They are now fairly

common. The United States Public Health
Service survey found them in 80 out of 95 of the
largest cities and the American Child Health
Association found them in at least 24 out of 86
smaller cities.

Standards for the open-air school are described in some detail by Warren (21). The
site is important. Ideally this will be in a
wooded location in the suburbs. But in crowded
sections where this is not feasible they are often
located on the top of a tall building. The classroom is usually either a shelter open on all sides
or else it has one side open to the weather. In
the former case the kitchen, dining room, and
bathrooms should be entirely enclosed and
heated. The children spend a long day in the
school. On arrival in the morning they bathe
and then are generally given special warm
clothing. The day is broken by lunches and a
rest period after dinner. The curriculum is especially planned not to overtax the weakened
bodies of the children and there are periods of
supervised mild exercise. A nurse stays with the
children while a physician visits them frequently. Where the open-air school is impossible
open-window classes are a fair substitute. These
are held in a regular classroom, the windows of

which are kept wide open, the children being equipped with special heavy clothing.

Another aid in school health work is the sight-conservation class. The United States Public Health Service survey of 1923 found such classes in at least 25 of the 100 largest cities, while the American Child Health Association found them in five out of 86 smaller cities in 1924. In the last few years the movement has been growing very rapidly. The National Society for the Prevention of Blindness knew of 292 sight-saving classes in 1927. It is felt that by the careful supervision given in these classes it is often possible to preserve the vision of the child who would otherwise become totally blind. This implies absolute coöperation between the teacher and the eye specialist. The room must be equipped with a perfect lighting system. The children should have special books printed in large type, raised maps, and special large blank books in which they write or print their lessons. Special classes for the blind child are also frequently found in our more progressive cities.

Cardiac classes are much less common. There would seem, however, to be a definite need for them. According to the Association for the Prevention and Relief of Heart Disease (quoted in 3) about 0.7 per cent of our school children have definite heart defects. That is to say 70 children in every thousand suffer from this handicap. Of these 70 about 64 are yet able to indulge in more or less strenuous physical activities. On the other hand the balance, or six children per thousand, should be permitted very little or no activity. It is for these children that the cardiac classes have been established. They must be held on the first floor of the school building to prevent the exertion of going up and down stairs. Play is carefully supervised to guard against sudden strain. School work is modified and an intensive effort is made to improve the child's health by hygienic measures.

Special classes for hard-of-hearing children are reported in at least 30 of the 100 largest cities by the United States Health Service survey and in nine smaller cities by the American Child Health Association. Here treatment will vary in accordance with the degree of the defect. The worst cases are given training in lip reading. Classes for crippled children are reported in about one-fourth of the 100 largest cities. They imply classes held on the ground floor of the building, arrangements for transportation and special classroom equipment, including specially constructed chairs and desks. The posture clinic (13) is a related development.

All of these efforts for child health will be of little use without the intelligent coöperation of the child himself. The school experience will have little effect on the child if his teachers have been unable to teach him health habits which will remain through later life. Therefore, there has been a commendable effort in recent years in the direction of health education. It is felt that the elementary laws of hygiene are at least as important in the child's life as history and geography. Although much has been accomplished much more remains to be done before the American child has adopted entirely satisfactory health habits. A survey of 35,349 fifth grade children by the American Child Health Association (1) showed that 39 per cent were in the habit of drinking coffee, that 22 per cent drank no milk, and that only 53 per cent had visited the dentist within a year.

It is with the hope of teaching these and similar habits that a great deal of emphasis has been placed in recent years on the subject of health education. The best educational thought is now unanimous in looking upon such teaching as a function of the school. The American Child Health Association found, however, that definite courses existed in only 66 out of the 86 cities studied.

Harman (11), studying state courses in health, reports a very great change in the last ten or fifteen years. Although many of the curricula still show an emphasis on unimportant anatomical details, the newer courses evidence an effort to bring the study into vital relation with the life of the child. The subjects receiving most emphasis in the newer courses are personal hygiene, physiology, and community health. The first of these subjects includes instruction in the elementary laws of hygiene such as the first principles of a good diet, the need of regular exercise and regular elimination, and the influence of mental attitude upon health. The course in physiology takes up the various systems and explains in simple language the functions of the body. Under the head of community health come such subjects as the control of epidemics, the principles of sanitation, and the elements of public-health administration. Other topics include first aid, baby care, mental hygiene, and the hygiene of the factory, home, and school.

Perhaps the most salient characteristic of modern health education is its insistence that the knowledge gathered be put into practice. It makes little difference that the child should be able to repeat the reasons for drinking milk if he continues to drink coffee at home. There is little to be gained from the knowledge of the advantages of cleanliness if the children do not apply this knowledge to their life. Therefore a number of devices have become popular to make the child practice these health habits.

One of the most usual of these is the use of weight charts. The child is weighed periodically and the results are recorded on a graph. While our confidence in the use of weight and height as an index of physical condition has been somewhat shaken by the studies quoted above, a sudden drop in weight or the absence of gain is a sign which ought not to be neglected. By creating a spirit of rivalry the teacher makes the children interested in their weights and when a pupil fails to gain as he should the teacher can make it a starting point for a talk on the necessity of good health habits.

Another scheme in common use consists of giving the child charts to record the practice of health habits. One popular plan is that provided by the Modern Health Crusade. Other charts have been originated by school systems themselves. The common feature of all these schemes is a chart on which the child and his teacher or

parents attest that he has been faithful to certain health habits, such as posture, cleanliness,
drinking milk, and sleeping a specified number
of hours per night. Sometimes a child is given
a mark on his monthly report card on this basis.
Another common scheme consists in encouraging the child to make health posters. In the
lower grades these may consist of pictures cut
out of advertisements or magazines and accompanied with simple legends of the child's own
composition. The results may be crude but the
fact that they were produced by the children
themselves is a very great point in their favor.

The school lunch is another aid in demon-
strating health habits. After all, there is no way
of teaching a child to drink milk quite so effectively as having him drink it in the classroom. In special classes for the tubercular and
other seriously handicapped children these
lunches are often replaced by full meals in
which the children may be taught many facts
of dietetics by actual practice.

Courses in physical education are among the
most effective means of inculcating health
habits. Since, however, the character-building
aspects of supervised play is being more and
more insisted upon, this topic is postponed to
the chapter on recreation.

Many people are beginning to realize that the home is a strategic point in the battle for child health. Without the coöperation of the parents it is very difficult to teach health habits. An appeal is therefore often made to them by having them present at the physical examinations, or through the medium of Parent-Teacher Associations, or by sending home to them health material such as posters made by their children.

The history of the child-health movement is the history of an effort to substitute prevention for treatment. The line of battle is being pushed constantly farther and farther back and the ounce of prevention is gradually taking the place of the pound of cure. If the school can succeed in its object of teaching positive health it ought to have a great influence on the men and women of tomorrow, for although physical health is not the highest of man's attributes it is nevertheless a most fundamental one. Health is essential for the fullest living and before a person can accomplish his work in the world it is necessary first of all that he be alive and reasonably well. Body and soul are intimately united and by the care of the former modern education can do much to aid the latter to attain to higher and higher accomplishments.

## BIBLIOGRAPHY

(1) American Child Health Association, Research Division: *A health survey of 86 cities.* New York, American Child Health Association, 1925. xxxiv, 614 p.
An excellent study of practice in cities of medium size.

(2) American Federation of Organizations for the Hard of Hearing: *The hard-of-hearing child.* Washington, D. C., U. S. Gov't Printing Office, 1925. vi, 72 p.   (Public Health Bulletins No. 110.)
Detection of defects, medical and surgical treatment.

(3) Baker, Sara Josephine: *Child hygiene.* New York and London, Harper & Brothers, 1925. xii, 534 p.
Probably the best book on the subject.

(4) Baker, Sara Josephine and Blumenthal, J. L.: "Methods of determining malnutrition." *Nation's Health,* 5:47-50, January, 1923.
Shows height-weight-age tables to be unreliable.

(5) Bridgeport, Conn., Board of Education—Division of Dental Hygiene: *Report of five years of mouth hygiene in the public schools of Bridgeport, Conn., Presented by the Division of Dental Hygiene of the Bridgeport, Connecticut Board of Education, Alfred C. Fones, Director of Dental Hygiene.* Bridgeport, Conn., 1921. 21 p. incl. cover title.
An outstanding experiment in school dental hygiene.

(6) Clark, Taliaferro, Syndenstricker, E. and Collins, S. D.: "Height and weight as an index of nutrition." *Pub. Health Rep.,* 38:39-58 January 12, 1923.

(7) Clark, Taliaferro, and Collins, Selwyn D.: *A synopsis of the child hygiene laws of several states including school medical inspection laws.* Washington, D. C., U. S. Gov't Printing Office. 1925. vi, 72 p. (Public Health Bulletins No. 110.)
An excellent compilation.

(8) Dublin, Louis I., and Gebhart, John C.: *Do height and weight tables identify undernourished children?* New York, Issued by the New York Association for Improving the Condition of the Poor, 1924. 23 p.
Answers this question in the negative.

(9) Eye Sight Conservation Council of America: *Eyesight conservation survey.* Compiled by Josua Eyre Hannum, edited by Guy A. Henry. New York, The Eye Sight Conservation Council, n. d. 219 p.
The most comprehensive survey of the subject.

(10) Fones, Alfred C.: *Seven years of mouth hygiene in the Bridgeport schools.* 7 p. (Reprint from *Dental Cosmos*, Oct. 1921.)
An account of the excellent work being done in Bridgeport.

(11) Harman, Hyra Hulst, and Clark, Taliaferro: *A study of courses in health education.* Washington, D. C., U. S. Gov't Printing Office, 1925. iii, 53 p. (Public Health Bulletins No. 152.)
A very excellent survey of the subject.

(12) Howe, William A., "School medical inspection in New York State." *Am. Jr. Public Health*, 15: 305-9, April, 1925.
Tabulates the results of physical examinations of 595,206 children.

(13) Klein, Armin: *Posture clinics; organization and exercises.* Washington, D. C., U. S. Gov't Print-

,,er

ing Office, 1926. v, 32 p. (Children's Bureau Publication No. 164.)

A brief, but rather comprehensive treatment of the problem.

(14) Newmayer, Solomon Weir: *Medical and sanitary inspection of schools for the health officer, the physician, the nurse and the teacher.* New York and Philadelphia, Lea & Febiger, 1924. x, 462 p.

A standard work on the subject.

(15) New York State Commission on Ventilation: *Ventilation; report of the New York State Commission on Ventilation.* New York, E. P. Dutton & Company, 1923. xxvi, 620 p.

This report has had a revolutionary effect on school practice.

(16) Roberts, Lydia J.: *What is malnutrition?* Washington, D. C., U. S. Gov't Printing Office, 1927. iv, 19 p. (Children's Bureau Publication No. 59 Revised.)

A brief, popular, yet authoritative *résumé* of the best knowledge of this subject.

(17) Rogers, James Frederick: *Better teeth.* Washington D. C., U. S. Gov't Printing Office, 1927. 19 p. (Bureau of Educ., Health Education No. 20.)

A short summary of some of the outstanding facts.

(18) Rogers, James Frederick: "Present status of school hygiene in the United States." *Am. Jr. Public Health,* 18:53-65, January, 1928.

A short but excellent review of the movement.

(19) Terman, Lewis Madison: *The hygiene of the school child.* Boston, New York, etc. Houghton Mifflin Company, 1914. xvii, 417 p.

Somewhat out of date, but still worth reading.

(20) U. S. Public Health Serivce: *Municipal health department practice for the year 1923 based upon*

*surveys of the 100 largest cities in the United States made by the United States Public Health Service in cooperation with the Committee on Administrative Practice, American Public Health Association.* Washington, D. C., U. S. Gov't Printing Office, 1926. xxiii, 782 p. (Public Health Bulletin No. 164.)
An excellent summary of health department work.

(21) Warren, B. S.: *Open air schools for the prevention and cure of tuberculosis among children.* Washington, D. C., U. S. Gov't Printing Office, 1919. 20 p. (Public Health Bulletin No. 58.)
Gives plans, blank forms, and other practical details.

(22) Winslow, Charles-Edward Amory: *Fresh air and ventilation.* New York, E. P. Dutton & Company, 1926. xi, 182 p.
A popular account of the results of the latest scientific research.

(23) Wood, Thomas D. and Rowell, Hugh Grant: *Health supervision and medical inspection of schools.* Philadelphia and London, W. B. Saunders Company, 1927. 637 p.
A large work containing accounts of the methods used in various places.

(24) Wood, Thomas D. and Hendrickson, Ethel M.: *Ventilation and health; the new hygiene of pure air.* New York and London, D. Appleton and Company, 1927, xvii, 201 p.
The application of the newer knowledge of ventilation.

# CHAPTER IV

## *The Problem of Delinquency*

Every year about one and one-half per cent of the children of juvenile-court age in our large cities are brought before the court. This number is very unevenly divided between boys and girls, about three to five times as many of the former as of the latter appearing on the court records. The age distribution is also very uneven, the percentage being very much higher for children over 13 than for children under that age. In the country districts the proportions are probably much lower.

It seems to be a very general impression that delinquency among children is rapidly increasing and that we are in the midst of a sort of crime wave. It is extremely difficult to get accurate statistics on the incidence of delinquency, but the United States Children's Bureau (1) announces that the best available information does not seem to support this belief. If anything, there appears to be a very slight decrease in juvenile delinquency during the last decade or two.

But even though there is probably no increase in the number of child offenders, the situation is in any case serious enough. The fact that between one and two per cent of our children fail so seriously to adjust themselves to life in the community that they must be cited before the court indicates a grave social problem. Various studies have shown that criminal careers can very frequently be traced back to youth. The reason why adult criminals have chosen their antisocial careers is that the ounce of prevention was lacking in their youth.

For these reasons the community is now thoroughly awake to the gravity of the problem of the juvenile delinquent. It is felt that the strategic point in the battle which the community must wage with crime lies back in the very beginning of the criminal's career. There is little hope of effecting a permanent reform in the character of a hardened criminal, whereas the young offender who is merely starting his life of crime offers much more promising material for treatment.

The differential treatment of the child offender goes back to the common law which presumed that a child under the age of seven was incapable of committing crime. Between the ages of seven and fourteen the child was regarded as having the possibility of discernment but the question of his responsibility might be raised and decided in accordance with the evidence. Beyond the age of 14 the common law recognized no distinction between the treatment of the child and the adult.

Some of the early colonial laws concerning children were rather grim. Thus we find a Connecticut law of 1672 providing that if any child above 16 years old and of sufficient understanding should "curse or smite his natural father or mother" such a child should be put to death (2). It must be remembered that such laws were not passed merely for possible exigencies but that they were actually enforced.

The spirit behind the early colonial legislation, either for children or adults, was dictated by the theories of Beccaria and other writers of the Seventeenth Century who founded what has been called the *classical school* of penology. According to this school the criminal commits his offense to secure a possible advantage. To stamp out crime it is only necessary for the community to attach penalties which will outweigh any possible advantage to be derived from the criminal act. The offender, weighing the possible advantages and the possible punishment would always choose the line of least resistance and would avoid crime if the penalties were sufficiently severe. Later modifications of this doctrine admitted that in the case of some persons, notably children and idiots, the theory would apply only partly, for such persons were incapable of judging the consequences of their acts. But in general Eighteenth-Century penology was based on the naïve assumption that crimes were committed after a deliberate weighing of the possible good and bad effects.

Early in the Nineteenth Century, sounder views on the nature of crime and punishment began to prevail, particularly as regards children. It was gradually realized that the juvenile offender presented problems of his own quite distinct from those of the adult. Later the whole classical theory began to be questioned. The offender is a complex human being quite different from the rationalizing abstraction postulated by the followers of Beccaria. A more human and humane view of his treatment began to be adopted.

One expression of this new feeling was the foundation of separate institutions for juvenile offenders. As early as 1812 John Stanford of New York had suggested the desirability of this, and in 1824 the New York Association for the Prevention of Pauperism incorporated a "House of Refuge," which was opened in the following year. A similar institution was founded in Philadelphia a year later and by the middle of the century a total of seven had been opened. In 1900 the United States Bureau of Education reported 88 such institutions.

This was paralleled by a tendency in various states to enact special legislation for the juvenile delinquent. For example, Illinois, in 1827, raised the common-law age of responsibility from seven to ten years and in 1833 prohibited the detention of persons under 18 in the penitentiary except for robbery, burglary, and arson. Others could be sentenced to a maximum of 18 months in the county jail.

Perhaps the most significant development in this field during the last century was the probation system. As early as 1849 John Augustus, a shoemaker of Boston, began his work as an informal probation officer in the Boston courts, but it was not until 1878 that the first probation law was passed in Massachusetts. No other state enacted similar legislation until 1899 (20).

It was not until the beginning of the present century, or in 1899 to be exact, that the juvenile court made its appearance—an institution which changed the whole aspect of the problem of juvenile delinquency. In that year the Illinois Juvenile Court Act was passed and the first session of the Cook County Court was held. Since that time the growth of juvenile-court legislation has been extraordinarily rapid. The Children's Bureau (3) reported that in 1918 all cities of over one hundred thousand had specially organized children's courts, although the country districts were much less favorably situated. At present all states except Maine and Wyoming have juvenile-court laws of some sort.

The juvenile-court movement is to some extent an outgrowth of the above-mentioned tendency to look upon the young offender as a special problem and to provide specialized treatment for him. But it is also an expression of a new and more scientific conception of the crime problem in general—a conception which goes back to the work of Lombroso dating from about 1876.

The theories of Lombroso are now regarded as definitely disproved, yet we must not lose sight of the fact that this investigator was the first to take a scientific view of the question of delinquency. He believed that the criminal represented a distinct and atavistic type, discoverable by anthropometric methods. This theory has failed to be confirmed when subjected to careful scientific analysis. However, the impetus which it gave to the scientific study of the criminal has lasted to the present time.

The years following Lombroso's work have seen many attempts to find some simple solution of the crime problem. At one time feeble-mindedness was looked upon as being the principal cause. At another, crime was held by many to be a form of insanity. At the present time, however, all these theories are recognized as fallacious. There is no simple explanation of crime. It is now realized that the causes of crime are as complex as the causes underlying any other species of human behavior. Almost anything which may influence human conduct may play its part as one of the causes of crime.

At present the emphasis is altogether upon the individual delinquent. Every offender presents his distinct problem and the juvenile court simply represents an attempt to study the case and to give the appropriate treatment.

This reflects a theory quite different from the criminology of the last century. In the traditional court the point was to establish the guilt or innocence of the offender and in case of his guilt to apply the punishment prescribed by statute. In the new, socialized court the emphasis is shifted from the offense to the offender. The question of his guilt or innocence becomes of minor importance and the dominant purpose of the court is to find what treatment is most appropriate for the particular problems of the delinquent. The motto of the old court was to make the punishment fit the crime but the motto of the new court is to make the punishment fit the criminal (7, 8).

Although it is now recognized that the causes underlying the conduct of each offender are exceedingly complex, yet it is profitable to inquire into the relative importance of the various factors which have to do with the causation of crime. At one time heredity was looked upon as being of supreme importance. Studies of individual families, as will be mentioned in another chapter, once captured the imagination of the country and it was believed that crime was largely a hereditary affair. Modern research has failed to substantiate this view. Specific moral traits cannot be handed down from generation to generation. Feeble-mindedness and certain physical defects may be hereditary but moral qualities are not. The "moral imbecile" thus becomes a chimera and we cannot expect eugenics to play a dominating rôle in the prevention of crime.

Neither can we attach much importance to

economic status. The criminal averages well below the economic mean of the general population but it is probably not true that he is a criminal because he is poor but rather that he is poor
because he belongs to the unadjusted type from
which criminals are recruited.

Somewhat more important are home conditions. Burt (5) made a careful comparative
study of a group of delinquents in London and
a group of non-delinquent children from a similar social stratum. He found that defective discipline and defective family relationships were
both much more frequent in his delinquent
group than among the others. The child coming
from a broken home or the child coming from
a home where discipline is defective is much
more likely to grow into a criminal than a child
from a normal home. Immorality in the home
naturally handicaps the child. The boy or girl
who is accustomed to the sight of open vice in
his home for many years offers promising material as a recruit for the ranks of the criminal.

Inexperienced social workers are apt to blame
bad companions in many cases for the misconduct of the child. This is a comforting explanation for the mother, who is thus able to shift
the blame of her child's misconduct to the shoul-
ders of the neighbor's child. It is an open ques-

tion, however, whether a boy becomes bad because he associates with bad companions, or whether he associates with the undesirable companions because he is himself potentially delinquent.

As will be stated in another chapter, unwholesome recreation in undesirable places is prominent in the etiology of crime. The child who has plenty of normal, healthy play is not likely to go astray, while the one with insufficient or improper forms of recreation is much more likely to become delinquent.

Physical defects are probably not as important as they were once considered (6). Serious students cannot any longer accept the naïve view that crime is merely a question of tonsils and adenoids or of defective glands. It may happen that the abundant physical energy of the overdeveloped boy or girl may lead to some misconduct or that the physically handicapped child may be at a disadvantage compared to his normal fellows, but in general it cannot be said that physical factors are very significant.

Mental defects are probably a more frequent cause of crime. Here we may distinguish two rather different types. The low-grade feebleminded child may actually be unable to distinguish between right and wrong and may be delinquent because of pure stupidity. The higher-grade defective will be able to distinguish between right and wrong, it is true, but he will be unable to appreciate the importance of motives that will impress the normal child and will often fail to see the danger of situations in which he allows himself to become involved.

Among the most important causes of crime are those which may loosely be grouped together under the head of personality defects. Only a small proportion of these reach the stage of legal insanity; but the fact remains that the most common concomitant of delinquency is an unstable, unadjusted type of personality. Crime is the weakling's attempt to find a short cut to happiness. Some of the modern knowledge of these defects and their treatment will be reviewed in the next chapter.

Finally, we must not forget that neglect of religion is the most fundamental cause of crime though this aspect of the subject does not belong in the present treatment.

The problem of delinquency thus reveals itself as an exceedingly complex one. It has no simple solution.

The modern socialized court represents an attempt so to modify our traditional legal machinery as to make this individualized treatment possible. This implies a freedom of procedure which was alien to the spirit of the old-time court. The procedure in most of the children's courts in the United States is chancery, and not criminal; that is, the delinquent is regarded rather as a ward of the state needing treatment than as an offender who must be punished.

The judge of such a court needs specialized training. The salary therefore should be liberal enough to attract competent men to the office. The tenure of office should be long enough and secure enough to allow the judge to develop a special interest in his work. For these reasons it is considered very bad practice to allow the judges of a court of general jurisdiction to occupy the juvenile court bench by turns. Such a system takes away all incentive to specialized preparation for the treatment of the problem of juvenile delinquency.

To insure the court proper freedom in its work its jurisdiction should include not only children definitely delinquent but also all those whose condition makes necessary the same sort of socialized care which the court secures for delinquent children. It should include also adults who are involved in any way in the child's delinquency. Juvenile courts also very frequently have jurisdiction over illegitimacy cases, applications for adoption, non-support or desertion of minor children, and the determination of the custody of homeless, abandoned, and destitute children. The age limit of juvenile courts in the case of children should not be less than 18 years and jurisdiction once obtained should continue until majority (16).

There has been a tendency in certain places to bring to court children guilty of very minor offenses. Not only is this unjust to the child, subjecting him as it does to undesirable humiliation, but also it has the disadvantage of crowding the docket and thus interfering with the proper treatment of more serious cases. The best practice is to have some sort of a preliminary hearing before the chief probation officer or some other court official who receives all complaints but who does not bring the offender before the judge for official action unless it appears that the nature of the case demands it. It is thus possible to adjust informally a large proportion of the cases. The best practice requires at least a summary investigation even of informal cases.

Once it has been decided that a case is serious enough to be brought before the judge, however, it should be studied carefully. The gathering of this information by the court is one of the characteristics of the juvenile court which differentiates it sharply from the old-fashioned type. If the treatment is to be made to meet the needs of the individual delinquent it is necessary for the judge to have before him a full report of the offender's problems. In the ideal case these preliminary investigations should include a study of the child's home conditions by a trained social worker, a physical examination by a physician, the administration of mental tests by a psychologist, and a personality study by a psychiatrist, as well as information concerning the delinquency or other condition leading to the child's appearance in court. This standard of thoroughness is found as a routine procedure only in the exceptional juvenile court; yet the majority of such courts approach it at least in a few of their most important cases.

Only infrequently will it be necessary to detain the child before the hearing. In these cases the child should never be sent to a jail or be detained in a police station. He should either be kept in a specially designed "house of detention" or else, as is done in Boston, he should be placed in a private family home. In a majority of cases, however, the parents can be depended upon to bring their child to court for the hearing.

The use of referees is a fairly common procedure in juvenile courts. Such referees have the power to hear cases and to dispose of them tentatively subject to confirmation by the court. It is thus possible to handle a larger number of cases than if the judge worked unaided. This is particularly true in rural districts where the area over which the court has jurisdiction is so large that the judges cannot easily cover it alone. The use of women referees in girls' cases involving sex offenses is now a very common procedure.

The actual court procedure in the socialized court represents a striking break with legal tradition. Instead of the usual courtroom the judge frequently hears cases in his private office or in some other small and simply furnished room. There is a minimum of formality and a minimum of publicity. The case is discussed in an informal manner and there is a happy absence of red tape.

The resources of the court for treatment are at least as important as those for the study of the case. The most important of these is probation, which has its legal justification in the power of the court to suspend sentence subject to certain conditions. As has been said above, probation antedated the juvenile court; but with the growth of the latter movement it took on a new importance. The probation officer represents an extension of the power of the court outside of the actual courtroom. He acts as a representative of the judge to see that the latter's orders are carried out. His rôle is not that of a police officer enforcing obedience, but that of a social worker alive to the complexities of human problems and able to notify the court when a modification of treatment appears necessary. To secure the type of person who can do this properly the probation officer should be adequately paid. Both his salary and his training should approximate, for example, the standard which we expect in the case of a high-school teacher. Otherwise these positions will not command the services of the proper type of men and women and thus the work of the courts will suffer.

No probation officer should be expected to supervise more than 50 cases at one time. Where a larger number than this is assigned to him, which happens in a great many courts, thorough work becomes impossible. Another important element in good probation work is the careful supervision of the work of the officers by someone who understands case-work standards. Finally, in order to give the court the background necessary for the further treatment of the case, all information gathered by the officers must be recorded systematically.

State supervising agencies have played a notable part in the improvement of probation work which has taken place in the last few years. Such agencies exist at present in at least nine states (16). Not only have they exerted a legal control or supervision over probation work, but—more important still—by their educational activities they have helped to interest the general public in the whole juvenile-court movement. Several states, through their general county programs for child welfare, have helped to make probation service available to the rural districts (17).

Even with the best probation work some behavior difficulties will not yield to this technique. In these cases the child may have to be removed from his own home. Sometimes he may be placed in a boarding home where the changed environment offers new possibilities of successful adjustment. More often, however, the child will have to be sent to an institution for delinquents. The best of such institutions have ceased to wear the aspect of prisons. The emphasis is no longer on punishment but rather on understanding the difficulties of the child and giving them the appropriate treatment (23). It must be admitted, however, that many of our institutions have not taken this more enlightened view of their function.

The juvenile-court movement is growing very rapidly. Not only is the number of these courts increasing but the type of work being done by them is being constantly improved. There is evident also a tendency to standardize and supervise their work. Two agencies have played a predominant part in this standardization; namely, the United States Children's Bureau and the National Probation Association. The former has made a number of studies of court practice which have had a vast influence on the whole movement. The latter organization was founded in 1901 and was known until 1911 as the National Probation Officers Association. It distributes information on juvenile-court work, makes studies and holds annual conferences, the proceedings of which are a mine of information on the whole problem of delinquency. The generally recognized standards of juvenile-court practice are those adopted in 1923 at a conference held under the joint auspices of these two organizations (21). Practically the same standards are embodied in the *Standard Juvenile-Court Law* which was drawn up by a committee of the National Probation Association and approved at the annual meeting of that body in 1925. (See appendix of reference 16).

In the last dozen years or so there has been an interesting tendency to give jurisdiction over juvenile delinquents and domestic relations cases to the same court. It is felt that the problems involved in both types of cases are the same and that it is therefore both difficult and unwise to separate them. It is as yet too early to say whether such combined courts will become the rule in the future, but they certainly represent an interesting development.

Besides the official treatment of delinquency which has thus far been the subject of this chapter an enormous amount of work is being done by non-court agencies. The school has been able to treat a number of cases through visiting-teacher work and well organized school-attendance departments. The possibilities of preventive work by the police are being utilized more and more by some cities. Ever since the time of Christ the Church has maintained an active interest in the delinquent. Volunteer workers have often been of great assistance as informal probation officers. The *Big Brothers* is a national organization which has done much to make such volunteer service available.

The juvenile-court movement represents a

definite break with the older ideas of penology
but it is only what we ought to expect as a result of the newer knowledge of the criminal.
Realizing as we do the complex nature of the
motivation which leads to misconduct, the logical answer is a court like the juvenile court in
which the individual delinquent is carefully
studied and then all the resources of the community are applied to the solution of his
problem.

## BIBLIOGRAPHY

(1) Abbott, Grace: "Trend in juvenile-delinquency statistics." *Jr. of Am. Inst. Crim. Law and Criminology*, 17:167-72, August, 1926.
Juvenile delinquency apparently not increasing.

(2) Bailey, William Bacon: *Children before the courts in
Connecticut.* Washington, D. C., U. S. Gov't
Printing Office, 1918. 98 p. (Children's Bureau
Publication No. 43.)
A scholarly treatment.

(3) Belden, Evelina: *Courts in the United States hearing
children's cases. Results of a questionnaire study
covering the year 1918.* Washington, D. C., U.
S. Gov't Printing Office, 1920. 115 p. (Children's Bureau Publication No. 65.)
Report of a questionnaire survey.

(4) Brill, Marian S.: "Motivation of conduct disorders in
boys." *Jr. Delinq.*, 11:5-22, March, 1927.
More motives are necessary to drive the brighter
children into delinquency.

(5) Burt, Cyril Lodowic: *The young delinquent.* London, University of London Press, ltd., 1925. xx, 643. p.
A most scientific study of the individual delinquent.

(6) Carter, William E.: "Physical finding in problem children." *Mental Hygiene*, 10:75-84, January, 1926.
Physical causes were of minor importance.

(7) Cooley, Edwin J.: *Probation and delinquency; the study and treatment of the individual delinquent.* New York, Catholic Charities of the Archdiocese of New York, 1927. xv, 544 p.
Report of an interesting experiment in adult probation.

(8) Gillin, John Lewis: *Criminology and penology.* New York and London, The Century Co., 1926. xii, 873 p.
A voluminous review of the subject.

(9) Glueck, Sheldon: "Psychiatric examination of persons accused of crime." *Mental Hygiene*, 11:287-305, April, 1927.
Experience with the Massachusetts law of September, 1921. There were 295 cases examined. Legal machinery for dealing with them is antiquated.

(10) Healy, William and Bronner, Augusta F.: *Delinquents and criminals, their making and unmaking; studies in two American cities.* New York, The Macmillan Company, 1926. viii, 317 p.
A study of the results of modern methods of treating delinquency.

(11) Healy, William: *The practical value of scientific study of juvenile delinquents.* Washington, D. C., U. S. Gov't Printing Office, 1922. 31 p. (Children's Bureau Publication No. 96)
A popular treatment.

(12) Johnson, Fred Robert: *Probation for juveniles and adults; a study of principles and methods.* New York and London, The Century Co., 1928. xiii, 242 p.
Very good. Gives case records.

(13) Judge Baker Foundation, Boston: *Case study no. 1-20 Series 1.* Boston, Judge Baker Foundation, 1922. v, pages not numbered.
Perhaps the best series of cases studied in existence.

(14) Lenroot, Katharine F. and Lundberg, Emma O.: *Juvenile courts at work; a study of the organization and methods of ten courts.* Washington, D. C., U. S. Gov't Printing Office, 1925. vii, 323 p. (Children's Bureau Publication No. 141.)
An excellent review of current practice. This study has played a very important rôle in the modern movement to standardize juvenile-court practice.

(15) Liepmann, M.: "American prisons and reformatory institutions; a report." *Mental Hygiene*, 12:225-315, April, 1928.
A translation by Dr. Fiertz of a report by Dr. Liepmann who visited the United States in 1926 as a member of a commission appointed by the city of Hamburg to study prison practice in this country.

(16) Lou, Herbert H.: *Juvenile courts in the United States.* Chapel Hill, The University of North

Carolina Press, London, H. Milford, Oxford University Press, 1927. xvii, 277 p.
The best review of the topic.

(17) Lundberg, Emma O.: *The county as a unit for an organized program of child caring and protective work.* Washington, Gov't Printing Office, 1926. iii, 25 p. (Children's Bureau Publication No. 169.)
Probation work is an important phase of these county child-welfare activities.

(18) Murchison, Carl Allanmore: *Criminal intelligence.* Worcester, Mass., Clark University, 1926. 291 p.
Contends that criminals do not average below normal in intelligence.

(19) Overholser, Winfred: "The psychiatric examination of prisoners in Massachusetts." *Boston Med. and Surg. Jr.,* 195:1065-67, December 2, 1926.
Deals with the Massachusetts law of 1921 requiring certain prisoners to be examined by a psychiatrist.

(20) Parsons, Philip Archibald: *Crime and the criminal, an introduction to criminology.* New York and London, Alfred A. Knopf, 1926. xvi, 387 p.
A good general introduction to the newer ideas in criminology.

(21) U. S. Children's Bureau: *Juvenile-court standards; report of the committee appointed by the Children's Bureau, August, 1921, to formulate juvenile-court standards, adopted by a conference held under the auspices of the Children's Bureau and the National Probation Association, Washington, D. C., May 18, 1923.* Washington, D. C., U. S. Gov't Printing Office, 1923. vi, 10 p. (Children's Bureau Publication No. 121.)

# THE PROBLEM OF DELINQUENCY 109

A fundamental document. Also printed as an appendix in (15).

(22) U. S. Children's Bureau: *Proceedings of the conference on juvenile-court standards held under the auspices of the U. S. Children's Bureau and National Probation Association, Milwaukee, Wisconsin, June 21-22, 1921.* Washington, D. C., U. S. Gov't Printing Office, 1922. 111 p. (Children's Bureau Publication No. 97.)
The work of this conference led to the standards of reference (21).

(23) Van Waters, Miriam: "Where girls go right; some dynamic aspects of state correctional schools for girls and young women."
*Survey Graphic* 1:361-76, June, 1922.
A popular treatment of the newer type of institution for delinquent girls.

# CHAPTER V

## *Mental Hygiene*

The greatest scourge which is threatening the health of the American people is not tuberculosis, nor pneumonia, nor disease of the heart. It is mental disease. There are almost as many patients in the mental hospitals of this country as in all other hospitals combined. From one-sixth to one-third of each state's total expenditures goes to the upkeep of these hospitals. Over seventy-two thousand men were rejected for mental and nervous diseases from the draft army. Even looked at from the purely physical side insanity is a fatal disease. A recent study by the Metropolitan Life Insurance Company (13) shows that at some ages the death rate of patients in the New York State mental hospitals is from 12 to 20 times as high as at the same ages in the general population of the state. Unlike many other diseases which are being successfully met by public-health measures, there is no sign that mental disease is on the decline.

Statistics for the year 1927 showed that for the thirty states studied there were 226.9 patients in state mental hospitals per one hundred thousand population as compared to 218.4 four years previously (19). From all points of view mental disease is a great and growing menace to the health and welfare of the American people.

Until a few years ago there seemed to be no effective way to combat this scourge. But what is often called "the new psychology" has given the psychiatrist a more hopeful insight into the problem. Whereas twenty years ago the care of patients in mental hospitals was largely confined to an effort to keep them physically healthy and to prevent them from injuring themselves or others, now, at least in our more progressive hospitals, distinct efforts are being made to treat and cure these conditions. What is still more hopeful is that the new methods have been used with apparent success to prevent these abnormal mental conditions in many instances.

Recent advances in the knowledge of the human personality have been responsible for the newer methods of treating mental disease. It is now known that unconscious motives play a very important rôle in human conduct. This knowledge is largely due to Freud and his followers. Whatever sins have been committed in the name of psychoanalysis this central discovery has certainly been of the greatest importance.

By the unconscious is meant the content of the mind which is not at the moment in consciousness. Evidently this must be very extensive. Of the myriad ideas which exist in a person's mind —recollections of childhood days, knowledge acquired in school, memories of persons and things—only a very small fraction can be actually in the focus of the mind at a given instant. The balance forms the unconscious.

All this is quite evident to anyone. The contribution which modern phychiatry adds to the above is the fact that these unconscious ideas can have a great, even a determining, influence on conduct. The man who has been badly frightened by a dog as a little child may have a lifelong prejudice against the canine species. There is no rational motive for this prejudice; it rests simply on an unconscious fear based upon a forgotten incident of childhood. So it is too with most of our irrational likes and dislikes.

A prejudice against dogs or rabbits, against a certain color, or a certain nationality, may not interfere seriously with conduct but in more extreme cases the unconscious motives may affect the major currents of a person's life. In such

cases the result may be anything from a trivial
queerness of character up to one of the major
psychoses. The man who has an irrational dis-
like for gray cats may never be seriously handicapped in the struggle for existence but the man
who has a fixed idea of his own inescapable inferiority evidently will be. Mental hygiene aims
to correct and prevent these abnormal mental
conditions.

The mental-hygiene movement has passed
through two distinct phases. In the first the emphasis was on the treatment of mental diseases;
in the second it has been on their prevention.
The former is represented by our mental hospitals and by neuropsychiatric clinics of the
older type. The latter, which forms the mental-
hygiene movement properly so called, is represented by clinics of the newer type and by certain educational measures.

The clinic has undoubtedly been the most effective weapon of mental hygiene. This is so
for two reasons. Not only has the clinic helped
to reduce mental disease through the actual
treatment of cases; but it has given a deeper
insight into the causes of these abnormal conditions, thus making possible more effective preventive measures. This phase of the movement
has developed very rapidly. In 1925 there were

approximately 400 mental clinics in the United States. Their number is constantly increasing.

The neurological clinic was the forerunner of the modern type. This institution was confined to the treatment of abnormal conditions with a definite organic basis. With the introduction of the newer methods of treatment for mental diseases these clinics began to widen their field and to accept cases where the cause of the disorder was psychic rather than organic. With this change of scope came a change of name and they began to be called psychiatric, or neuropsychiatric clinics.

A new development has been the clinic for problem children. Such centers are known under various names, but the term "child-guidance clinic" has become fairly well standardized to describe this particular type. It differs from the neuropsychiatric clinic in that it works with children rather than with adults and confines itself to minor problems of conduct.

The experience of psychiatrists has pointed convincingly to the importance of the earliest years of childhood in the formation of personality. This has been the reason of a still newer development—the habit clinic. This type is concerned with the treatment of minor disorders in pre-school children. It represents one of the most promising developments in the field (21).

It is not yet fully apparent what form of overhead organization will ultimately become dominant among mental clinics. Those already organized show as astonishing variety. They are sponsored by institutions and agencies of all sorts and there is as yet no agreement about which arrangement is preferable.

As has been the case in many other progressive movements the pioneer clinics were generally organized under private auspices. An outstanding example of such work is furnished by the demonstration clinics sponsored by the Commonwealth Fund in connection with its five-year Program for the Prevention of Delinquency beginning in 1921. This particular part of the program was administered by the National Committee for Mental Hygiene through its Division on the Prevention of Delinquency. Demonstration clinics were opened in a number of cities and they were so successful that permanent, locally supported, clinics were established in seven cities. Besides this, aid was given through field consultant service leading to the opening of clinics in three other cities (3).

Very frequently clinics have developed from the out-patient service of some general hospital.

Special hospitals for mental diseases often offer clinical service along similar lines. Such clinics have been particularly valuable in two ways They are able to treat patients whose condition is not serious enough to warrant commitment to a hospital, and they can exercise a continuing supervision over patients discharged from the mental hospital. At first these clinics were predominantly of the neuropsychiatric type mentioned above. That is to say, they were more concerned with serious mental conditions of adults than with the conduct disorders of children. But there has been considerable overlapping, particularly in recent years. It is reported (10) that nearly a half of the patients of the Boston Psychopathic Hospital and the State Psychopathic Hospital of Iowa are children.

A rather recent development has been the clinic connected with a social agency. The best available statistics seem to indicate that about a third of the cases coming to the attention of family welfare agencies involve some problem of mental disease or defect. Since the agency cannot deal with these families effectively without giving attention to the psychiatric aspect of the case many feel that it would be useful if the agency included a mental clinic as a part of its organization. This plan has already been put into successful operation in some places.

Although the work of privately organized clinics is very important, probably the most significant feature of the movement at present has been the rapid development of clinics organized under public agencies. In this field very excellent work is being done by clinics connected with state mental hospitals. Usually these are not housed in the hospital itself on account of the unpleasant associations which such institutions still have in the mind of the public. Instead they are usually held at convenient points in the community at a general hospital or in some public building. There has recently been a very distinct effort to bring the benefits of this service to the rural districts. This is accomplished by traveling clinics, the staff of which holds consultations at centers in the rural districts as the need arises.

Of equal importance is the court clinic. The modern treatment of delinquency focuses attention on the personality of the offender and the clinic offers the best means for studying this intensively (9). It is not surprising, therefore, to find that nearly all courts of the modern socialized type are in the habit of availing themselves of clinical service. Sometimes the court includes a clinical staff within its own organization.

Sometimes offenders are sent from the court to some outside clinic for examination. The former represents the better practice, provided that the clinic is adequately staffed.

A development closely related to the above is the psychiatric examination of prisoners. The most significant piece of legislation in this connection is the Massachusetts law passed in 1921 and since twice amended which requires the clerk of court to report to the state Department of Mental Diseases all persons accused of a capital offense and all persons indicted or bound over for a felony who have previously been convicted of a felony or previously indicted for any other offense more than once (7). Upon receiving this report the Department sends two psychiatrists to examine the prisoner and their report is available not only to the court but to the district attorney and to the counsel for the accused. The plan seems to be giving general satisfaction.

Since the school is the one institution which comes into contact with practically all the children of the community, it would seem to be logical to establish clinics as part of the school system. It would thus be possible to reach problem children in their earliest years. In spite of the logical force of this argument, however, there are to date few school clinics and these few are largely supported by private funds in coöperation with the school department. The success of the clinics in Newark, New Jersey, has proved the feasibility of the publicly supported school clinic (5). The possibilities of psychiatric work in high schools have been shown by the five-year demonstration in a New York City high school sponsored by the Girls' Service League of America (8).

It may be seen from the above that the development of the mental clinic has been a bit sporadic. The present state of the movement may be gathered from the report of the survey of municipal public-health work in the hundred largest cities of this country conducted by the United States Public Health Service (22). Of the cities from which information was obtained, 27 reported that they had no mental clinics. There were 44 cities which possessed one or more mental clinics held "at frequent and regular intervals." In 16 others clinical service was available "occasionally or irregularly." Of the 60 cities which had some form of service all but 15 reported that their service included both diagnosis and treatment. There was a striking lack of uniformity in the overhead organization of these clinics. They were attached to juvenile and probate courts, boards of education, out-patient departments of various public or private health and welfare agencies, including children's-aid societies, mental-hygiene societies district nursing associations, and so forth.

Whatever the scope of a given clinic, whether it serves adults, school children, or children under school age, and whatever the body may be which sponsors it, certain general principles and methods will apply. The object of the clinic is to study the individual. For this purpose a number of recent techniques are called into play. To obtain a complete picture of the patient and the causes of his maladjustment it is necessary to investigate his physical condition, his social background, mental caliber and his personality make-up. This implies the services of a physician, a specially trained social worker, a psychologist, and a psychiatrist. Besides these persons it may be necessary to employ an office executive and one or more stenographers to take charge of the office and keep the records.

The general plan of procedure is also fairly well standardized. The child may be referred to the clinic by his parents, school, a court, or some other social agency. If the parents bring the child in person the history of the child's trouble is obtained from this source. If the case is referred by a social agency a detailed statement generally accompanies the letter of reference.

After this procedure the child is examined by a physician to locate any physical causes which might figure in his difficulty. In the meantime a specially trained social worker studies the patient's home and neighborhood background. A psychologist administers mental tests to determine the degree of the subject's intelligence. Finally the psychiatrist himself interviews the child. The findings of the other members of the clinic are generally made available to the psychiatrist in written form before the interview so that he may be in a position to make a diagnosis intelligently upon the case.

More important still is the treatment. This naturally takes different forms, according to the nature of the case. In clinics where psychoanalysis is practiced frequent visits over a long interval may be indicated. In other cases it will be necessary merely to give the patient himself or his parents insight into the trouble to effect a cure. More often, however, the treatment will be carried out by the social worker under the direction of the psychiatrist and will extend over a considerable period of time. In many clinics it is customary to hold case conferences at frequent intervals, the various members of the clinic bringing their experience to bear on the treatment of a particular case.

The above represents the accepted standard of practice in the mental clinic. It is a standard, however, which many clinics fail to attain. Sometimes family-welfare agencies carry on the treatment in the absence of specially trained psychiatric social workers. Sometimes a psychologist takes the place of the psychiatrist on the staff, in which case the clinic should confine itself to cases of intellectual abnormality. There are occasional clinics, too, which are operated for private gain and among these are some whose ethical standards are open to criticism.

The emphasis in clinical work is constantly shifting in the direction of prevention. Whereas the older neurological or neuropsychiatric clinics were concerned exclusively with patients suffering from a definite mental disease the newer clinics—particularly the child-guidance and habit clinics—seek to meet the trouble in its early stages, before it has become serious.

Another example of the tendency to reach the problem child as early as possible is the visiting-teacher movement. The visiting teacher is a social worker with a teaching background who

is attached to a school and whose work is to deal
with conduct disorders interfering with the
child's school efficiency. The movement began
in 1906, when two settlement houses, one in New
York and one in Boston, each set aside a social
worker to coöperate with the local schools. In
the following year the Public Education Association of New York appointed several more.
In 1913 New York City appointed six visiting
teachers whose salaries were paid out of the
public funds. From that time on the movement
has continually grown. Much of the recent
growth is due to the action of the Commonwealth Fund, which sponsored several demon-
strations of visiting teacher work in connection
with its Program for the Prevention of Delinquency. The visiting teacher must have both
teaching experience and case work training. She
is thus in a position to interpret the standpoint
of the case worker to the school and to explain
the school's viewpoint to the social agencies with
which she comes into contact. Oppenheimer (16)
in a nation-wide study of the movement found
very various arrangements for the overhead organization of visiting-teacher work. In some
cities it was strongly centralized under the direction of the superintendent of schools or some

other central agency, while in other cities the opposite tendency was evident and each worker was assigned to one school or group of schools.

As has been said, the visiting teacher concerns herself with the minor problems of the school child. The above study by Oppenheimer showed that about one-third of the problems reached were school problems. About one-fourth had reference to home conditions. Next in order came conduct, attendance, and health problems. The most common method of treatment was personal supervision, which was the principal measure used in about one-third of the cases. In about one-fourth the coöperation of other social agencies was enlisted to solve the problem. Medical treatment and family case work were dominant measures, each in about one-seventh of the cases. It may be judged from this that the visiting teacher can be a valuable help in preventing conduct disorders before they have become serious enough to be brought to the clinic. This has been the experience of the cities which have tried out this form of preventive work.

Another aspect of preventive work includes measures of a general educational nature. The organization most active in this field has been the National Committee for Mental Hygiene founded in 1909 (2). This body, with headquarters at New York, acts as a clearing house for information having to do with mental disease. It publishes pamphlets and books as well as a quarterly magazine, *Mental Hygiene*, and a monthly *Mental Hygiene Bulletin*, devoted to the general subject of mental disease and its treatment. The committee has also made a number of surveys in various states showing the need for better facilities for the care of the mentally ill. It furnishes information to state legislatures and interests itself in the passage of constructive measures in this field. The activity of the National Committee for Mental Hygiene in connection with the Commonwealth Fund Program for the Prevention of Delinquency has already been mentioned. The work of this national body is paralleled by the activities of various state societies which do within their own territory the same general type of work which the national committee does for the nation as a whole.

Since many serious mental illnesses can be traced back to unwholesome habits formed in childhood it is extremely important that parents be taught to train their children intelligently in their earliest years. The mother who gives in to her baby when he cries is training him to cry when he meets difficulties instead of trying to overcome them himself. The father who beats his child when the latter acknowledges a fault is teaching the child to be dishonest.

One hopeful way of reaching the parent is by means of parenthood education. In a previous chapter this movement has already been mentioned. To fulfill the requirements of mental hygiene, however, it must be modified in two respects. Existing courses in the care of the child which are being given to high-school or college students are concerned almost exclusively with the requirements of physical care. It is the contention of the leaders of the mental-hygiene movement that the training of the personality is even more important than the care of the body. Again, these courses have been given almost exclusively to girls. For the success of the movement it is necessary that the future fathers be taught as well as the future mothers. For the efficient training of the child depends on the active coöperation of both parents.

There is yet another way in which the school can coöperate with the mental-hygiene movement. The experience of the mental clinic has been that a very large proportion of all cases of mental trouble have their origin in matters of sex. The unfortunate attitude of society on this subject is such that the child who has had sex experiences or premature knowledge is filled with shame and a feeling of inferiority. He is afraid to discuss his troubles with any adult because previous questions on his part have been greeted with expressions of horror and disgust. Thus are sown the seeds for what may later become serious mental trouble.

Many good people are opposed to systematic sex instruction because they feel that such teaching prematurely destroys the innocence of the young. There is a great deal to be said for this view. However, all available studies show that where instruction is not given in a proper way children acquire this knowledge themselves from undesirable sources at a very early age.

A number of questionnaire studies have been made on the frequency of auto-erotic practices among men. They were made under conditions insuring anonymity so that there was little reason for the subjects to give false information. In two groups studied by Exner (6) 61.5 per cent and 34.7 per cent of the men admitted having such practices. Peck and Wells (18) found a proportion of 92.4 per cent, while Achilles (1) obtained a figure of 74.4 per cent from a small group of Columbia students. A striking thing about these studies is the fact that most of the subjects reported having begun the practice before the age of 15 years. This was true of 69.6 per cent in Exner's group, 54.3 per cent in Peck and Wells' group and 68.3 among Achilles' subjects.

Several studies along similar lines dealing with girls have been reported. Achilles (1) obtained a figure of 45.2 per cent from a group of college women. Davis (4) reported that 64.8 per cent of a group of one thousand unmarried women and 40.1 per cent of a similar number of married women had formed this habit. Here again the ages at which these practices commenced was strikingly early. In the three groups which are referred to, 61.5, 60.0, and 69.4 per cent, respectively, commenced the habit before the age of 15.

These studies are somewhat open to criticism because they deal with selected groups, usually college students or college graduates. But we have no reason to assume that they are not fairly typical of the population as a whole. The conclusion to be drawn is quite plain. Children acquire sex knowledge and sex practices very early in life. This being the case, it is futile to talk about preserving the innocence of the young. Whether we like it or not the children will acquire such knowledge from random sources. We cannot guard them against this knowledge. We can decide, however, whether they shall be allowed to acquire it from evil-minded persons or whether it shall be given them decently by someone they can love and respect.

It would certainly be the ideal thing if parents would assume this responsibility. There is a certain sacredness about the home which makes the treatment of these topics both safe and natural. Experience has shown, however, that parents in general shirk this responsibility or postpone it until the damage has been done. Many, therefore, feel that it will become a responsibility of the school. The United States Public Health Service (22) reports that in the 100 largest American cities 25 are making definite efforts in the field of sex education. Fourteen other cities report some slight activities, while the balance have made no move in the matter. Whatever method will ultimately be found the most feasible, there can be no doubt about the urgency of the problem. If all our children could be taught to regard these subjects sanely and purely it would certainly mean a great simplification of our mental-hygiene problem.

It will be seen from the above brief survey that we have today scarcely scratched the surface of the mental-hygiene question. The leaders of the movement dream of a day when the resources of the community will be focused on the problem with a substantial decrease in mental disease and a corresponding increase in human happiness.

## BIBLIOGRAPHY

(1)   Achilles, Paul Strong:  *The effectiveness of certain social hygiene literature.*  New York, American Social Hygiene Association, 1923.  50 p.
A study made under the auspices of the Committee on Evalution of Social Hygiene Literature of the American Social Hygiene Association.

(2)   Barker, Lewellys F.:  *The first ten years of The National Committee for Mental Hygiene, with some comments on its future.*  New York, The National Committee for Mental Hygiene, 1922.  25 p.
A review of the early accomplishments of this remarkable organization.

(3)   Commonwealth Fund:  *Ninth annual report for the year 1926-1927.*  New York, The Commonwealth Fund, 1928.  78 p.
Includes an account of the Fund's program in mental hygiene and child guidance.

(4)   Davis, Katharine Bement:  "A study of certain auto-erotic practices based on the replies of 2,255 women to questionnaires prepared by the Bureau of Social Hygiene with the advice of a cooperative committee."  *Mental Hygiene,*  8:668-723 and 9:23-59, July, 1924 and January, 1925.
A very detailed analysis.

(5) Dexter, Elizabeth H.:  "Treatment of the child through the school environment."  *Mental Hygiene,*  12:358-65, April, 1928.

An account of the work of the Newark Public
School Child Guidance Clinic.

(6) Exner, Max Joseph: *Problems and principles of sex
education; a study of 948 college men.* New
York, Association Press, 1915. 39 p.
Gives questionnaire data on sex practices.

(7) Glueck, Sheldon: "Psychiatric examination of per-
sons accused of crime in Massachusetts." *Mental
Hygiene*, 11:287-305, April, 1927.
How the Massachusetts law of 1921 works out.

(8) Greene, Elizabeth: "Results of five years' psychiatric work in New York City high schools."
*Mental Hygiene,* 11:542-57, July, 1927.
Results of psychriatric work in New York City
high schools sponsored by the Girls' Service League
of America.

(9) Healy, William: *The practical value of scientific
study of juvenile delinquents.* Washington, D. C.,
U. S. Gov't Printing Office. 1922. 31 p. (Children's Bureau Publication No. 96.)
Shows how the services of the mental clinic can
aid the juvenile court.

(10) Jarrett, Mary C.: *Mental clinics; an account of
their development in the United States.* New
York, National Committee for Mental Hygiene,
1927. 57 p.
An excellent review of the mental clinic—its background and present status.

(11) Joint Committee on Methods of Preventing Delinquency: *Three problem children; narratives from
the case records of a child guidance clinic.* New
York, Joint Committee On Methods of Preventing Delinquency, 1924. 146 p.
A readable account of three actual cases.

(12) Lou, Herbert H.: *Juvenile courts in the United States.* Chapel Hill, The University of North Carolina Press; London, H. Milford, Oxford University Press, 1927. xvii, 277 p.
A standard reference on juvenile courts.

(13) Metropolitan Life Insurance Company: "Mortality of patients in hospitals for mental diseases." *Statistical Bull. Met. Life Ins. Co.,* 9 (5):1-3, May, 1928.
Compares by sex and age the death rates of the population of New York State mental hospitals 1914-1923 with the corresponding figures for the general population of the state 1919-1920.

(14) Moore, Thomas Verner: *Dynamic psychology; an introduction to modern psychological theory and practice.* Philadelphia, etc., J. B. Lippincott Company, 1924. viii, 444 p.
A good introduction to the newer psychology.

(15) Morgan, John Jacob Brooke: *The psychology of the unadjusted school child.* New York, The Macmillan Company, 1924. xi, 300 p.
An excellent popular treatment of the principles of the mental hygiene of childhood.

(16) Oppenheimer, Julius John: *The visiting teacher movement, with special reference to administrative relationships.* Second edition. New York, Joint Committee on Methods of Preventing Delinquency, 1925. xvii, 206 p.
A careful study of the movement in 1923.

(17) Peck, M. W. and Wells, F. L.: "Further studies in the psycho-sexuality of college graduate men." *Mental Hygiene,* 7:697-714, October, 1923.
A questionnaire study.

(18) Peck, M. W. and Wells, F. L.: "On the psycho-

sexuality of college graduate men." *Mental Hygiene,* 7:697-714, October, 1923.

"The individuals discussed . . . constitute some three-quarters of a group of almost 250."

**(19)** Pollock, Horatio M.: "State institution population still increasing." Mental Hygiene, 12:103-12, January, 1928.

Based on the preliminary results of the first annual census of state institutions. Includes data on admissions during 1926 and the population on January 1, 1927.

**(20)** Smith, Geraldine Frances: "Certain aspects of the sex life of the adolescent girl." *Jr. Appl. Psychol.* 8:347-49, 1924.

A study of 171 college girls.

**(21)** Thom, Douglas Armour: *Habit clinics for the child of preschool age; their organization and practical value.* Washington, D. C., U. S. Gov't Printing Office, 1924. v, 71 p. (Children's Bureau Publication No. 135.)

An account of guidance work for the young child written by a pioneer in the field.

**(22)** U. S. Public Health Service: *Municipal health department practice for the year 1923 based upon surveys of the 100 largest cities in the United States made by the United States Public Health Service in cooperation with the Committee on Administrative Practice, American Public Health Association.* Washington, D. C., U. S. Gov't Printing Office, 1926. xxiii, 782 p. Public Health Bulletin No. 164.)

An excellent survey of public-health practice in large cities.

# CHAPTER VI

## *The Bar Sinister*

It is only in the present century that the problem of the illegitimate child has been systematically attacked in America. This is certainly most unfortunate. For the problem is important not merely on account of the number of children who thus enter the world severely handicapped but also on account of its value as an index of underlying social wrongs.

It is difficult to estimate the number of illegitimate children born every year in the United States. Lundberg (9) estimated that the figure was about fifty-eight thousand in 1923. The Census Bureau reports that according to its records 2.40 per cent of the births in the Registration Area in 1926 were illegitimate.* But this probably very much understates the case. Births have never been recorded in this country with the exactness which is found in Europe, where the completeness of birth records has an impor-

* Personal communication to the author.

tance from the standpoint of military service. Even in our Registration Area a certain percentage of births are never recorded and presumably a large proportion of these unrecorded births represent children born out of wedlock.

The situation in the United States is not as serious as it is in Europe where the rate for 1926 was higher than that of the United States in 14 out of 15 countries for which comparable statistics were available (6). The Netherlands furnished the one exception, reporting a rate of 1.89 per cent. However the problem is serious enough even here and it ought to arouse the sympathy and interest of every public-spirited citizen.

One reason for the importance of the problem is the extremely high infant mortality rate among illegitimate children. Our data are sadly incomplete but the figures we have are startling enough. We know for instance that Baltimore in 1915 had an infant mortality rate of 294.2 per thousand live births for children of illegitimate birth as compared with the rate of 102.0 for other children (14). Another study in Boston for the year 1914 gives a rate of 251.4, or 2.4 times the general rate (11). The same study reports figures from a large institution in which the annual rate was 421. In certain foreign countries the data are very much more complete than in America. We know for example that in the period 1910 to 1914 the rate was at least twice as high among illegitimate as among legitimate children in the Netherlands, Norway, France, England, and Wales; and in all European countries it was at least 30 per cent higher according to statistics compiled by the United States Children's Bureau (10) from figures furnished by the *Institut International de Statistique* (5). More recent data are not available to the present writer except in the case of England where for the five-year period ending 1926 the mortality rate was 1.89 times as high among illegitimate as among legitimate children (2). If there were no other reasons for being interested in the problem of illegitimacy it would be important merely as a public-health problem and this aspect alone would more than justify all the pains we have taken to attack it.

Exact information on the whole illegitimacy problem in the United States is unfortunately lacking. However, in the last few years a number of careful studies have been made under the supervision of the Children's Bureau. There was the Baltimore study of 1914 (14), the Massachusetts study in six sections (11), and the five so-called *schedule studies* (17). Most of the information in the following pages is summarized from these sources.

A striking fact brought out by these studies is the extreme youth of the mothers. Averaging the results from the twelve studies above listed we find that 4.0 per cent of the mothers were under 16; 13.6 per cent were between 16 and 18; and 30.5 per cent were between 18 and 21. In other words about one-half of these girls had not yet attained their majority. It will be seen therefore that the problem we are considering is particularly a problem of youth.

An effort was also made to learn something of the previous character of the parents. Nine studies for which the information is given show that from one-fourth to two-thirds of the mothers were known to have been previously delinquent or of poor character. In one study (11) where an effort was made to gather similar data concerning the fathers it was found that about two-thirds of them were also of poor character.

The mothers are distinctly below the average mentality. A study made by Lowe (8) included the mothers of all illegitimate children born in seven maternity hospitals during a specified period. All were tested whom it was possible to test. It was found that about two-thirds of the mothers had intelligence quotients of under 95, while 23.84 per cent had intelligence quotients below 75 which means that something like a fifth of them must have been feeble-minded. Somewhat less critical are the data from 11 Children's Bureau studies. In these it was known that about one-eighth of the mothers were either "feeble-minded, subnormal, or insane." Another one-twelfth were probably normal while the rest were either normal or else their mentality was unknown.

Another striking fact revealed by these studies is the unsatisfactory home life of the girls who became the mothers of illegitimate children. Only about one-half of them came from normal homes. The remainder had at least one parent dead, or the parents were divorced, separated, or deserted. Of the unmarried mothers who were not living in their homes it was known that about one-third of them had left home before the age of 14 and another one-third between 14 and 18. It seems safe to assert that the home life of these girls must have been very poor. It was undoubtedly characterized by a lack of vital religious training.

In one study about six-sevenths of the mothers were gainfully employed at the time of the birth of the child and in another about nine-tenths of them were.

From these studies we can picture the type of the unmarried mother. She is a girl of somewhat less than the average mentality coming perhaps from a broken home who has left home early and has had to shift for herself.

There are two principal methods of attacking the problem of illegitimacy. One is through constructive legislation and the other is through well conducted social work. Both of these are necessary. It has been shown by experience that the best legislation is of little use in this particular problem unless it is backed up by good case work. The unmarried mother hesitates about bringing her condition to the notice of the public authorities and thus much good legislation remains unused. On the other hand excellent case work is rendered abortive by the absence of laws insuring the rights of the illegitimate child.

The whole legal attitude towards the unmarried mother and her child has been highly vindictive (3). Under the English common law which has had so much influence in this country the child was considered *filius nullius* and there was no legal relation between him and his mother. As a result he did not share in the legal benefits which the ordinary child derives from his family. Nor could he be legitimized by the subsequent marriage of his parents.

This attitude expressed the disgust of the community in the presence of a grave social evil. The newer attitude by no means condones the offense but it believes that the sin of the father should not be visited too literally upon the child who has been entirely innocent. Besides this, it is realized that even with the most favorable legislation both the mother and the child are bound to suffer in any case and it seems needlessly cruel to add to the suffering which is imposed upon them by circumstances.

Most of our modern illegitimacy legislation can be traced back to the Norwegian Laws of 1915 which were passed largely through the work of Johan Castberg (12). These laws provide for the immediate reporting of all illegitimate births. Upon receiving the report the State immediately starts proceedings to establish paternity. A feature of the process is that the burden of proof is placed upon the putative father so that unless he can prove the contrary he is considered the father of the child. Another radical change from former methods is the provision that both parents may be called upon to contribute to the support of the child and that this amount is to be proportional to the economic status of the more favored parent. The parents must, therefore, not merely give enough money to assure the child common physical comforts but enough to support him in the style to which the other sons of the more favored parent had been accustomed. The law provides also that in matters of inheritance the child receives exactly the same treatment as the legitimate offspring.

In the United States the beginning of real modern legislation on this subject is furnished by the Minnesota law of 1917. While this was much less radical than the Norwegian Law it was evidently inspired by the latter. At the same time the Inter-City Conference on Illegitimacy was turning the interest of socially minded people to this problem. Two great regional conferences were held in 1920 under the auspices of the Children's Bureau as a result of which the National Conference of Commissioners on Uniform State Laws was asked to prepare a model illegitimacy act. This body responded by appointing a committee to study the question and on their recommendation the *Uniform Illegitimacy Act* was adopted by the Conference at its San Francisco meeting in 1922. The Uniform Act as adopted fell very far short of the Norwegian law. It was felt that public opinion had not at that time reached the point where a more radical form of legislation would be favorably received. Therefore, in its present form the act deals exclusively with the establishment of paternity except for one section which provides that the condition of the child's birth shall not be noted on certificates of birth. The principles of this law were accepted in 1923 by four states, North Dakota, South Dakota, New Mexico, and Arizona, and by Iowa in 1925.

Present legislation shows startling variations, some states being very progressive, although most of them are still governed by old-fashioned views on the subject (16). Proceedings to establish paternity are allowed in all states except Louisiana, Texas, and Virginia. Such proceedings may be either civil or criminal in nature. The Uniform Act allows both and attempts to combine the advantages of each. This principle is embodied in the legislation of a few states. The usual procedure for the establishment of paternity is as follows. The mother makes a complaint before or after the birth of her child to a judge or magistrate having the power to commit for trial. The latter issues a warrant against the person named in the complaint and orders him to appear at a hearing. If there is sufficient evidence against him at this preliminary action he is brought up for trial which takes place after the birth of the child and at which a jury may generally be demanded. If the judgment is against the defendant, provision is made for the maintenance of the child, generally through periodical payments, and the father is required to give bond. Some states allow an appeal and others do not.

There are very great variations in state legislation in regard to the father's obligation. A few states are entirely without legislation on this point. Where laws exist and the amount to be paid is expressed, the sum varies from a minimum of a dollar a month in Arkansas to a possible 500 dollars a year in Oregon and the time during which it must be paid from three years in Tennessee to support until majority in Arizona. Many of the states leave the amount to be paid to the discretion of the court. Minnesota has made it a punishable offense if the father of an illegitimate child leaves the state before or within 60 days after the birth of the child. If he leaves with intent to evade proceedings he is guilty of felony and may be imprisoned two years. It is believed that the law would be hard to uphold in a court of appeal on account of certain technical difficulties. The Uniform Act secures the same results by a sounder method. It provides that the judgment of one state may be sued upon and made a domestic judgment in another.

Evidently there is a great deal of room for improving our American legislation in regard to support. A compilation by the author of the data in eleven Children's Bureau studies shows that 70 per cent of the fathers gave no support at all and only 13.6 per cent made continuing contributions. In about three-fourths of the cases no court action at all was reported and proceedings for support were made in only three-fifths of the remaining quarter.

The mother generally becomes the guardian of the child with rights to the child's earnings. The father generally has no right of guardianship but Illinois gives it to him after the child is ten years old. In most states the father can adopt the child with the mother's consent. The mother generally inherits the property of the child if he dies intestate. Legislation in regard to inheritance varies a great deal between state and state. Nearly all states give the child the right to inherit directly from his mother but only a few recognize his right to inherit through her. The right to inherit from the father is less often given. Arizona greatly simplifies the problem by providing that the illegitimate child shall have the same right to inherit as the legitimate child.

There are three possible ways of legitimizing

illegitimate children. Arizona and North Dakota simply provide that all children are the legitimate children of their natural parents. Again certain classes of children may have their status determined by law. Children born of marriages which have been declared void for such reasons as nonage, idiocy, racial differences, and so forth are generally provided for by law. In the South children born of marriages between colored and white are in many cases declared illegitimate by law. Where a common law marriage is recognized the children are, by common law, legitimate. Other provisions exist in the statutes of various states. Still a third form of legitimation is that which arises from the action of the parents. Nearly all states provide for legitimation in case the child's parents subsequently marry. A few states permit legitimation by the father without marriage. Sometimes this is done by court action, sometimes merely by rather informal acknowledgement.

As has been remarked in the beginning of this chapter even the best legislation is quite useless unless it is enforced. In some European countries as notably in Norway, the State authorities assume responsibility for putting the law into effect and the matter is thus not left to the attention of the mother or of social agencies. In the

United States this principle has not, as yet, been widely accepted. A notable exception is provided by the Minnesota law in accordance with which the State Board of Control is required to take appropriate steps to establish the paternity of and to provide for the support of any illegitimate children reported to it. To do this the law provides that "the Board may initiate such legal or other action as is deemed necessary; may make such provisions for the care, maintainance and education of the child as the best interests of the child may from time to time require and may offer its aid and protection in such ways as are found wise and expedient to the unmarried woman approaching motherhood. . . . . This chapter shall be liberally construed with a view to effecting its purpose, which is primarily to safeguard the interests of illegitimate children and to secure for them the closest approximation to the care, support and education that they would be entitled to if born of lawful marriage, which purpose is thereby acknowledged and declared to be the duty of the State." (Minnesota Law 1917 c. 194, sec. 2)

Good social case work is particularly necessary for the protection of the unmarried mother and her child. This requires first of all that contact with the mother be established as early in pregnancy as possible. For without such contact it is impossible to provide proper prenatal care which is so essential for the physical health of both mother and child. In this way also arrangements may be made for proper confinement care.

Even more important is the aftercare of the mother and child, especially from the standpoint of mental hygiene. Here two possibilities exist. Either the mother may remain with her child or the two may be separated. Modern standards require that the mother and child be kept together where this is at all possible. Particularly during the nursing period the child and its mother should not be separated except for the gravest reasons. A Maryland law of 1916 forbids the separation of mother and child until the latter is six months old except under specified conditions. Somewhat similar legislation was embodied in a North Carolina law of 1917 and in South Carolina laws of 1923 and 1924. A similar principle is expressed in a joint resolution of the State Board of Control and the State Board of Health of Minnesota, adopted in 1918, which, however, applies only to maternity hospitals.

In spite of the best efforts of those concerned it is sometimes quite necessary for the good of the child that it be separated from its mother.

Such is the case particularly when the mother is too young to care properly for her child or when she is insane, diseased, or feeble-minded. In any case the social agency responsible for the placement should give careful supervision to the mother and child as long as it is needed.

Where the child is placed out with the mother most successful results have been obtained when the mother was able to remain in her own home with the child. This however is an arrangement which is obviously not often possible. The plan of putting the mother and child in the former's parental home can be recommended only in those cases in which the girl's parents themselves are known to be proper guardians.

An old system which was very largely used was to secure domestic employment for the mother and place the child with her. Careful follow-up studies, however, show that this arrangement seldom brings entirely satisfactory results. It has been estimated that the mother of a young child can give only about half of her time to her work. For the welfare of the child she ought to devote the other half of her time to its care. It is difficult to find socially-minded employers who are willing to accept this necessary arrangement. Good homes in the families of relatives or friends seem seldom to be available.

Very frequently kind-hearted people are willing to take in the mother for a brief period but the arrangement is temporary and is generally doomed to failure. A modern plan whose possibilities are just beginning to be realized is the placement of mother and child in a boarding home. A small sum is paid to cover their maintainance. This, of course, is the principle of foster home care for the dependent child. It has worked out so successfully with them that it seems to be worth trying in the case of the unmarried mother.

In those instances where it was necessary to separate the child from its mother various plans of procedure present themselves. The old idea was to place such children in an institution. The modern conception of the place of the institution, however, is that it is an agency to be used only in special cases for children who need specialized care. As a corollary of this the institution is sparingly employed by the best modern social agencies in the case of the illegitimate child.

Placement in the mother's parental home seems to succeed in those cases and those alone in which the grandparents are willing and competent to undertake the responsibility. Another possibility is the father's parental home, a placement which offers interesting possibilities but which has seldom been used in the past. The present tendency is to place the child which must be separated from its mother in a boarding home. Adoptive homes are used with caution.

It will be seen that the problem of the illegitimate child is an exceedingly complex one which is only gradually being solved. However, great progress has been made in the past few years and it is to be hoped that in the next decade or two we will reach a really adequate solution to this pressing problem.

## BIBLIOGRAPHY

(1) Connecticut Child Welfare Association: *Study of children born out of wedlock in Connecticut.* Connecticut Child Welfare Assoc., 1927. 48 p. The group of 655 children born out of wedlock who were included in this study were known to social agencies in the State of Connecticut during the year 1923.

(2) England, Registrar-General: *The Registrar-Generals' statistical review of England and Wales for the year* 1926. (*New Annual Series, No.* 6) *Tables. Part I. Medical.* London, His Majesty's Stationery Office, 1927. iii, 493 p. A very thorough summary of vital statistics.

(3) Freund, Ernst: *Illegitimacy laws of the United States, analysis and index.* Washington, D. C., U. S. Gov't Printing Office, 1919. 98 p. (Children's Bureau Publication No. 42.)

Now somewhat out of date. Includes tabluar anal-
yses of laws.

(4) Grigg, Julia: "Illegitimacy as shown by a study of
the birth certificates from Franklin County in
1924." *Ohio Welfare Bull.* 3 (3) :1-8, March,
1927.
A study of the problem in a rural county.

(5) Institut International de Statisque—Office Perma-
nent: *Annuaire international de statistique. II.
Mouvement de la population (Europe).* La Haye,
W. P. Van Stockum & Fils, 1917. xviii, 182 p.
Contains comparative statistics of infant mortality
among legitimate and illegitimate children.

(6) Institut International de Statisique—Office Permanent: *Apercu de la démographie des divers pays
du monde.* La Haye, W. P. Van Stockum & Fils,
1927. xvii, 329 p.
A standard source of information on vital statistics.
It supercedes (5).

(7) Kammerer, Percy Gamble: *The unmarried mother;
a study of five hundred cases.* Boston, Little
Brown, and Co., 1918. xv, 342 p.
Treats the question from the psychological standpoint.

(8) Lowe, Charlotte: "The intelligence and social background of the unmarried mother." *Mental Hygiene*, 11 :783-94, October, 1927.
One of the best studies on the subject. It is based
on a group drawn from seven maternity hospitals.

(9) Lundberg, Emma O.: *Children of illegitimate birth
and measures for their protection.* Washington,
D. C., U. S. Gov't Printing Office. iv, 20 p.
(Children's Bureau Publication No. 166.)
The best short, popular, summary.

(10) Lundberg, Emma O. and Lenroot, Katharine F.:
*Illegitimacy as a child-welfare problem. Part* 1.
*A brief treatment of the prevalence and signifi-*
*cance of birth out of wedlock, the child's status,*
*and the State's responsibility for care and protec-*
*tion Bibliographical material.* Washington, D.
C., U. S. Gov't Printing Office, 1920,   105 p.
(Children's Bureau Publication No. 66.)
A review of the whole problem.

(11) Lundberg, Emma O. & Lenroot, Katharine F.:
*Illegitimacy as a child-welfare problem. Part* 2.
*A study of the original records in the city of Bos-*
*ton and in the state of Massachusetts.* Washington, D. C., U. S. Gov't Printing Office, 1921.
408 p.   (Children's Bureau Publication No. 75.)
One of the best available sources.

(12) Magnusson, Leifur:   *Norwegian laws concerning*
*illegitimate children.* Washington, D. C., U. S.
Gov't Printing Office, 1918.   37 p.   (Children's
Bureau Publication No. 31.)
An interesting account of this exceedingly signifi-
cant legislation.

(13) Reed, Ruth:   *Negro illegitimacy in New York City.*
New York, Columbia, Univ. Press, 1926.   136 p.
Case study from 500 cases in New York social
agencies.

(14) Rochester, Anna:   *Infant mortality; results of a field*
*study in Baltimore, Md. based on births in one*
*year.* Washington, D. C., U. S. Gov't Printing
Office, 1923.   400 p.   (Children's Bureau Publication No. 119.)
Includes a study of the infant mortality rate of
the illegitimate.

(15) Rosenberg, Rena and Donahue, A. Madorah:   *The*
*welfare of infants of illegitimate birth in Balti-*

*more, as affected by a Maryland law of 1916 gov-
erning the separation from their mother of children under 6 months old.* Washington, D. C., U.
S. Gov't Printing Office, 1925. v, 24 p. (Children's Bureau Publication No. 144.)
An excellent study. The law was found to cause
a sharp decline in infant mortality.

(16) Stevenson, Marietta: Analysis and tabular summary
of state laws relating to illegitimacy in the United
States in effect January 1, 1928 and the text of
selected laws. Washington, D. C., U. S. Gov't
Printing Office, 1929. (Children's Bureau
Chart No. 16.)
The source of most of the information on state
laws presented in this chapter.

(17) U. S. Children's Bureau: *Illegitimacy as a child-
welfare problem. Part 3, methods of care in
selected urban and rural communities.* Washington, D. C., U. S. Gov't Printing Office, 1924. xi,
260 p. (Children's Bureau Publication No. 128.)
These studies show the possibilities of case work
with unmarried mothers.

# CHAPTER VII

## *The Subnormal Child*

Society has always been conscious at least dimly of the problem of mental deficiency. In different ages the community's attitude has been widely different. In ancient times the laws of Lycurgus condemned the defective to death. The Christian Era in general has been characterized by a more tolerant attitude. The feeble-minded were looked upon as being objects of pity. At times indeed these unfortunates have been regarded with a sort of superstitious awe and it has been stated that the great Tycho Brahe kept an idiot as his constant companion whose mutterings he regarded as a sort of oracle.

It was not, however, until almost the beginning of the last century that any attempt was made to meet the problem of the defective in a scientific manner. The incident which brought this question sharply before the attention of the public was the discovery of the "Savage of

Aveyron" by sportsmen hunting in the Department of Aveyron, France, in 1798. This savage was a boy of probably 11 or 12 years who was roaming through the woods like an animal, feeding upon acorns and nuts, fighting with his teeth, having no articulate language, and running often on all fours.

This discovery immediately excited the attention of the learned world, on account of its bearing on the problem of the relative importance of heredity and environment. Itard, professor at a school for deaf mutes in Paris, undertook to educate the boy in order to prove that his deficiency was due to lack of training. After five years of the most painstaking work Itard was forced to confess that his attempt had been a failure and the boy was an idiot incapable of profiting by much training.

The French Academy, however, recognized the importance of Itard's work better than did the latter himself. For the painstaking work of the master had taught the child to recognize objects, to speak a little, and even to grasp the rudiments of reading and writing. The importance of this work was that for the first time in history a feeble-minded child had shown some response to systematic training.

Edward Seguin, a pupil of Itard, was also

quick to grasp the significance of his master's work and he became the founder of what has been called the *physiological method* of education for defectives. He opened in Paris in 1837, the first successful school to be instituted for the express purpose of educating defective children. His method postulated that all the highest intellectual processes depend on sense perceptions and that by educating the senses systematically it would be possible to raise the whole mental level of the defective. In 1848, at the time of the revolutionary disturbances in France, Seguin emigrated to America where he became identified with the beginnings of the movement to educate defectives in this country.

Before very many years the defects of the physiological method became apparent. The theory of the early schools was that they would restore their feeble-minded pupils to normality and return them to the community. It was soon seen, however, that this was an impossible hope. Important improvements in the condition of the pupils of these schools were made, it is true. They profited by sense-training, and became more amenable to discipline, and more able to care for themselves. There was no evidence, however, of general intellectual improvement and the illusory nature of the hope that they might become normal citizens was very soon recognized. In consequence these early institutions which were founded as temporary training schools gradually took on the characteristics of institutions for the permanent custodial care of the feeble-minded.

The prevailing feeling during the opening years of the present century was not only that the feeble-minded were incurable but that they were a very grave and threatening menace to the community.

The reasons for this prevailing pessimism was furnished by a series of studies of which the first was Dugdale's (4) account of the "Jukes" first published in 1877 and reprinted in 1910. It was a history of the progeny of five notorious sisters. A total of 709 individuals were known to have descended from these five women. Of these, 180 had been cared for by the public authorities either in the poorhouses or by outdoor relief. Besides this there were 140 criminals of various sorts, 60 thieves, 50 prostitutes, and 40 women venereally diseased. It was estimated that the care of these people over a period of 75 years cost the state something like $1,308,000.

Dugdale's study was the first of a number of similar investigations of which one of the most striking was Goddard's (7) study of the "Kalli-

kaks." This famous family has been characterized as an "experiment of nature." Martin Kallikak had an illegitimate son by a feeble-minded
girl whom he met in a tavern during the Revolutionary War. There were 480 descendants of
this illegitimate union, of whom 143 were known
to be feeble-minded, 46 were known to be normal, while the rest were of unknown mentality.
This progeny included 36 illegitimate children,
33 persons sexually immoral, 24 confirmed al-
coholics, 3 criminals, and 8 who kept houses of
ill-fame. Later on Martin Kallikak married a
normal girl and of the 496 direct descendents of
this union only three were known to be somewhat degenerate but there were no mental defectives. They were considered fine citizens,
prominent in public affairs, and eminent in social and political life.

The findings of the two studies mentioned
above were paralleled by the history of the
"Nams" (6) and the "Hill Folk" (2), the
"Piney's" (9), and the family of "Sam Sixty"
(10). All of these seemed to indicate that the
feeble-minded were an extraordinarily grave
social menace and that their condition was in-
exorably determined by heredity. Since it was
felt that nothing could be done to improve their

condition the country passed through an alarm-
ist period in which the most radical methods for
meeting the problem were seriously discussed.
The feeling of this period is typified by the report of the Committee to Study and to Report
on the Best Practical Means of Cutting Off the
Defective Germ-Plasm in the American Population. After considering the various methods to
meet the problem the Committee finally recommended segregation and sterilization as the most
feasible means to use. In the general alarm a
number of states hastened to pass sterilization
laws, beginning with the Indiana law of 1907.

This stage of pessimism was succeeded by a
period of reaction. It began to appear that the
laws of heredity did not operate with the mathe-
matical certainty that had been expected. The
study of the "Hill Folk" by Danielson and Davenport (2) in 1912 showed that the offspring
of the union of two undoubtedly feeble-minded
persons did not, as had been expected, yield 100
per cent of defective offspring, but only about
77 per cent. It was gradually realized that although feeble-mindedness was in general hereditary its laws allowed a certain amount of variation. The offspring of feeble-minded persons is
indeed generally below the average of the gen-

eral population. However, individuals among these may be quite normal or even above the average.

It was realized, too, that families such as the Jukes and the Kallikaks were altogether exceptional ones. It was but natural that in the early period of the study of this problem these very exceptional families were the first to receive attention because it was they who had given most trouble to the public authorities. But it gradually became known that there were other families whose members were quite as mentally deficient as the Jukes and Kallikaks yet who had given comparatively little trouble to the community at large.

The discovery of what we may call the *socially acceptable* feeble-minded was brought about during the second decade of the century as a result of the test movement.

It was indeed the problem of educating the defective which gave the original impetus to mental testing. The Paris school authorities had decided to establish special classes for defective children and they called upon two well-known physicians of that city, Doctors Binet and Simon to recommend methods of selecting children for these classes. These two men, realizing the futility of existing methods of diagnosing feeble-mindedness, proceeded to develop the first intelligence tests of the modern type. Previous to this, tests had been suggested only for various minor abilities, such as memory, reaction time to physical stimuli, or other minor functions. The distinctive thing about the Binet-Simon method was that it boldly attacked the higher mental processes at once.

As arranged by Binet shortly before his death in 1911 the scale consisted of four or five tests at ages from three years to adulthood. A child of six years for instance was expected among other things to be able to distinguish between morning and afternoon, to copy a diamond, and to count successfully 13 coins. A scale of this sort made it possible to define feeble-mindedness in quantitive terms, and the concept of *mental age* (MA) was introduced. For instance if a child is said to have a mental age of eight years it means that whatever his real, or chronological age (CA) may be, he is able to pass the tests about as well as the normal child of eight.

The Binet tests were soon introduced into the United States and various translations and adaptations were made. It was soon realized, however, that the tests were in need of considerable revision. Some of the questions were too hard for the ages to which they were assigned, others were too easy. As a result Doctor Terman undertook to revise it, and after extensive work finally issued the *Stanford Revision of the Binet-Simon Scale,* or more briefly the *Stanford Revision* (12). This scale, first published in 1916, is still the standard for work among the feebleminded. In the years which have passed many defects have become apparent. But in spite of these no better scale has been devised to date.

Like the original Binet scale the Stanford Revision contains tests for successive years from the age of three to the "superior adult." Every test successfully passed gives the child a certain number of months credit. These being added together give his mental age. The mental age divided by the chronological age is the intelligence quotient (IQ) which will be 1.00 (more generally written 100) for a child exactly normal, above 100 for the bright child, and below 100 for the dull. A special advantage of the intelligence quotient technique lies in the fact that the IQ is approximately constant. A child five years old who has an MA of four years will have an MA of approximately eight years at the age of ten, and of twelve years at the age of 15. In other words his IQ will be 80 at all three ages and remains a constant quantity characteristic of the individual in spite of his varying chronological age. At some age, probably between 14 and 16, mental growth stops and the intelligence quotient technique must be modified. But for the younger child it has been found that in spite of certain technical objections the method works out very well in practice.

The World War saw the application of intelligence testing on a large scale to recruits. Since the Binet-Simon tests and their various revisions required about an hour of a trained examiner's time to administer to an individual it became apparent that they could not be used in the Army where whole companies had to be tested at one time. Necessity proved the mother of invention and a committee of psychologists developed *Army Alpha* and *Army Beta*, the first really successful group tests. These could be administered to a whole company of recruits about as quickly as the Binet tests could be administered to a single individual. Since the war a large number of group tests have been developed to meet the needs of the school in testing children of various ages. For application to subjects too young or too defective for the Binet tests and for speech defectives *construction* tests have been devised. These are tests requiring manipulative skill. For example wooden blocks to be assembled into a picture are used.

For work with the feeble-minded, individual tests of the Binet type have become standard. It is thus possible to define feeble-mindedness in terms of IQ instead of by the merely descriptive definitions of the preceeding period. Although definitions vary somewhat among different authorities it has become a fairly universal practice to classify as feeble-minded any person with an IQ less than 70. The feeble-minded are divided again into morons, imbeciles, and idiots. The first of these classes includes feeble-minded persons whose IQ lies between 70 and 50. The second includes those whose IQ lies between 50 and 20 or 25 while the idiots form the lowest grades with IQ's varying down almost to zero.

The extensive application of the test method in schools, colleges, and institutions brought about a realization of the fact that feeble-mindedness was much more common than had been supposed. Previous to this time the only feeble-minded who had been studied very extensively were the ones in institutions, persons, in other words, who had shown an inability to adapt themselves to civilized society. With the application of the test method an altogether different type of defective came to light. It was the feeble-minded person whose intelligence was perhaps just as retarded as was that of the institutional case but who had proved able to adapt himself quite satisfactorily, though naturally in a humble way, to life in a modern community. The realization of this fact gave the death blow to the theories of the alarmists. The Jukes and the Kallikaks were finally seen in their proper light and a new and more hopeful period had opened.

The modern view of feeble-mindedness contrasts sharply with both of the theories which have been outlined above. During the period of physiological education, it will be remembered, feeble-mindedness was looked upon as a definitely curable condition. The inaccuracy of this view is now quite generally admitted. Certain very special conditions such as cretinism may yield to the proper treatment but in general modern science has little hope to offer for the improvement of the intelligence of the defective. But although the optimism of Seguin and his day has proved illusory we realize now that the pessimism of a generation ago is equally unjustified. While it is impossible to improve the mentality of the defective it is, at least in a very great many cases, possible to adjust him to normal society. Twenty years ago it was felt that segregation in an institution was the only appropriate treatment for the defective. It is now felt that while this is indeed true of the lowest grade of the feeble-minded, yet most morons and even imbeciles can be trained to occupy an honorable and self-respecting place in the community.

The modern attempt to solve the problem of the feeble-minded begins in the school. The dull child has suffered unnecessarily in the past from our attempt to make him keep up with the class work of his normal fellows. The test movement has shown us how impossible this is and the best modern schools make a conscious effort to adapt the curriculum to the needs of the individual child. Without going into details here it may be mentioned that it has been felt possible so to organize the classroom that each child may work approximately at his own pace, the bright doing more and the dull less, than the average child of the class.

The above arrangement will probably care for the higher grades of dull children. But no known system is flexible enough to handle in one classroom the bright, the normal, and the definitely feeble-minded. It is therefore recognized that below a certain point it is necessary to have special classes for dull children and such classes now appear in nearly all progressive school systems.

Details of organization vary widely. In some systems the defectives are taught in special classrooms in the same school building with the normal while in others special schools for the defective are housed in their own buildings. Methods of instruction also differ widely. But the underlying principle is the same, to give the defective child as much of the three R's as he is able to assimilate and after this point to give him manual work designed both as a method of sense training and as a preparation for a vocation.

This implies the organization of small classes of not more than 15 pupils under the care of specially trained teachers. It implies consequently a considerable added expense. Yet it is felt that it is not only more merciful but in the long run more economical as well to give the child the specialized training which may help to make him a useful member of the community rather than to allow him to develop into an institutional defective.

In spite of these developments it still appears impossible to care for all the feeble-minded children in the community in a day school and the institution is still recognized as an essential element in our answer to the problem of feeble-mindedness. In fact the number of inmates of such institutions is constantly increasing. In 1904 institutions handled 17.5 inmates per one hundred thousand general population, in 1910 the figure had increased to 22.5, in 1923 it was 39.3 (14) and we know that it has increased considerably since that time (11).

The modern institution recognizes quite consciously two different types of inmates. There is the type which on account of extraordinarily low-grade intelligence, or on account of undesirable character traits, gives no hope of being able to live in the community. Evidently the low-grade idiot who cannot feed himself, who cannot walk, talk, or guard himself against ordinary physical dangers will never be able to lead a normal life in the community at large and there will probably always be feeble-minded persons, even of the higher grades, whose personalities make it unwise to release them into the community, no matter how carefully their environment may be controlled. There remains, however, the type of feeble-minded child who has proved unable to make successful adjustments, even after attendance at a special day school, yet who offers hope of becoming a useful member of the community after a period of training in an institution. Many of these may even be of a definitely delinquent type, yet the modern institution holds that such cases can profit by appropriate treatment.

This is made possible by two things. First, by the effort on the part of the institution to train its inmates for successfful adjustment to group life. Although the feeble-minded offer little hope for profiting greatly from instruction in the common school subjects, they may be taught certain things. They may be taught, for example, hygienic habits and simple trades. It may require as much effort on the part of the teacher to train a feeble-minded boy to dig a ditch with even sides as it would take to teach an ordinary college student differential calculus; yet this time and effort will not be wasted if such simple accomplishments will make it possible for such a boy to take his humble place as a self-supporting and respected member of the community. The possibility of successful vocational adjustment in many cases is shown by the studies of Bryne (1), Ecob (5), Unger (13), and Kinder and Rutherford (8).

A second tendency has been the parole system, often used in connection with the colony idea. The development of the latter was chiefly due to Doctor Bernstein of the Rome State School for Mental Defectives at Rome, New York. Although the colony plan was in use sometimes even in the last century, Doctor Bernstein has developed it to such a degree that this method has been justly identified with his name. It is used in the modern institution for boys who have shown promise of eventually being able to adapt themselves to the community. These are placed in groups of perhaps 20, under supervision, on small farms, not too distant from the institution. If the child shows himself able to make adjustment in the colony he is permitted to return to the community, first under careful supervision, and later altogether free.

The colony for boys is paralleled by the colony for girls, which generally consists of a house in town where the girls live under careful supervision, and from which they go to work every day either as domestic servants or as factory operatives.

The colony plan furnishes the transition between the highly artificial life of the institution and the normal life of the community. Many who would not otherwise be capable of making successful adjustments are able to do so by means of the colony plan.

On the other hand the colony plan has certain disadvantages. It takes the feeble-minded away from the institution and consequently away from its expert staff of teachers, physicians, psychologists, and social workers. It makes difficult or impossible any systematic academic training.

The modern answer to the question of feeble-mindedness varies according to the degree of mental defect. For the highest grades of mental defectives the school itself can provide an answer, either by making an adjustment in the ordinary classroom or by the use of special classes. For the lower type of defective and for the defective delinquent the institution must be used, but with the hope of ultimate release and adjustment to the community in view. Finally there will always be an irreducible minimum of subnormals for whom permanent custodial care is the only satisfactory treatment. But it is no longer felt, as it was once seriously contended, that the only thing to do with the defective is to segregate him from society. The scale of human occupations varies in difficulty by imperceptible degrees from the highest to the lowest just as does intelligence; and there is, even in our modern world, work to do for all grades of intelligence except the very lowest. For the world needs its hewers of wood and drawers of water just as it needs its research scientists and captains of industry.

BIBLIOGRAPHY

(1) Bryne, May E.: "After-school careers of children leaving special classes in Minneapolis." *Ungraded* 10:75-86, January, 1925.

"It may therefore be safe to assume that about 40 per cent of the subnormal children of this community may·be considered as capable of doing work for wages."

(2) Danielson, F. H. and Davenport, C. B.: *The Hill Folk; report on a rural community of hereditary defectives.* Cold Spring Harbor, New York, 1912. v, 56 p. (Eugenics Record Office. Memoir No. 1.)

A study of a degenerate family.

(3) Davies, Stanley P.: *Social Control of the feeble-minded; a study of social programs and attitudes in relation to the problems of mental deficiency.* New York, The National Committee for Mental Hygiene, 1923. 222 p.

A historical survey.

(4) Dugdale, Richard Louis: *"The Jukes", a study in crime, pauperism, disease and heredity; also further studies of criminals.* Fifth edition, New York and London, G. P. Putnam's Sons, 1895. viii, 120 p.

A study of a degenerate family.

(5) Ecob, Katherine G.: "Mental defectives in the community." *Ungraded,* 9:125-32, March, 1924.

Follow-up of cases from records of New York State Commission for Mental Defectives.

(6) Estabrook, A. H. and Davenport, C. B.: *The Nam family; a study in cacogenics.* Cold Spring Harbor, New York, 1912. iii, 85 p. (Eugenics Record Office. Memoir No. 2.)

A study of a degenerate family.

(7) Goddard, Henry Herbert: *The Kallikak family; a study in the heredity of feeble-mindedness.* New York, The Macmillan Company, 1919. xv, 121 p.
A study of a degenerate family.

(8) Kinder, Elaine F. and Rutherford, Elizabeth J.: "Social adjustment of retarded children: a follow-up study from January to June, 1926, of retarded children seen in the Henry Phipps Psychiatric Clinic. *Mental Hygiene*, 11:811-33. October, 1927.
The subjects of study were 97 children brought to the clinic in 1921, at ages from 2 to 15 years, chiefly connected with social problems.

(9) Kite, E. H.: "The Pineys." *Survey*, 31:7-13, October 4, 1913.
A study of a degenerate family.

(10) Kostir, M. S.: *Family of Sam Sixty.* Columbus, Ohio Board of Administration, 1916. 29 p.
A study of a degenerate family.

(11) Pollock, Horatio M.: "State institution population still increasing." *Mental Hygiene*, 12:103-12, January, 1928.
A review of the latest statistics.

(12) Terman, Lewis Madison: *The measurement of intelligence; an explanation of and a complete guide for the use of the Stanford revision and extension of the Binet-Simon intelligence scale.* Boston, New York, etc., Houghton Mifflin Company, 1916. xviii, 362 p.
The original reference on the Stanford Revision.

(13) Unger, Edna W.: "Vocational training for subnormal girls; an experiment in the garment machine operating trade." *Jr. Pers. Res.* 5:243-55, October, 1926.

The possibilities of adjustment after specialized training.

(14) U. S. Bureau of the Census: *Feeble-minded and epileptics in institutions* 1923. Washington, D. C., U. S. Gov't Printing Office, 1926. 194 p.
In 1923 there were 42,954 inmates in institutions for feeble-minded in U. S. or 39.3 per 100,000 population.

(15) Wallin, John Edward Wallace: *The education of handicapped children.* Boston, New York, etc., Houghton Mifflin Company, 1924. xiv, 394 p.
An excellent reference on dull children.

(16) Whipple, Helen Davis: *Making citizens of the mentally limited; a curriculum for the special class.* Bloomington, Illinois, Public School Publishing Company, 1927. vi, 374 p.
A study of the curriculum for the dull.

# CHAPTER VIII

## *Recreation*

The last twenty-five years have seen very radical changes in our attitude towards play. A generation ago the expression "child's play" was used as a synonym for something trivial. Now, however, enormous sums of money are being spent both by private organizations and by public authorities for the systematic promotion of recreation.

This changed attitude has come about through the realization that play has an important effect upon character, that the child who does not play is to that extent handicapped, and that lack of sufficient opportunity for recreation is an important cause of delinquency.

It used to be assumed that the school was an adequate solution for all the problems of childhood. It was felt that formal education was a sufficient means of training the growing child in citizenship; but with the beginning of the present century, when the juvenile-court movement began to focus public opinion on the socially unadjusted child, it was gradually realized that the school actually plays only a small part in the child's life. The United States Bureau of Education (15) has reported as a result of careful study that the average school child in the United States actually attends school only about 131 days per year. Assuming a five-hour school day this means that the average time the child spends in school is only about one hour and three-fourths per day.

The time spent in the school, therefore, does not loom large in the child's life. But the time spent at play does. A child may occupy eight or ten hours a day in sleep, a couple of hours for his meals, washing, dressing, and so forth, and possibly, on a liberal estimate, he may occupy a couple of hours with work and chores. But it would be an extremely conservative statement to say that the average child of school age has about eight hours a day of relatively unoccupied spare time.

The above estimate is not pure theory. For instance, Johnson (9) studied 915 elementary school children in Cleveland on a pleasant Saturday and Sunday in June and found that they were spending about nine hours and forty-five minutes a day in play. The fact that so much

more time is spent at play than is spent in school
is one demonstrated fact which has caused socially-minded people to pay continually more
and more attention to the recreational problems
of the child.

A number of careful surveys have attempted
to determine what the child does in these hours
of spare time. The Newark Survey (12) may
be cited as typical of the best modern recreational studies. It was found that in this city the
street was by far the most common recreational
agency. Two out of every three eight-year-old
boys cite the street or vacant lot as their usual
playground. The same seems to be equally true
of older and younger children. Of the twenty-
six thousand school boys in that city only one-
sixth belong to adult-organized clubs.

The poverty of our children's recreational life
has been shown repeatedly. To summarize briefly a number of studies, about one-half of the children who have been observed in the course of
recreational surveys were found to be doing
nothing. They were simply sitting about idling,
waiting for something to turn up. About one-
sixth of them were working, either in street
trades or doing chores, and only about one-third
of the total number were observed to be actually playing.

Wholesome recreation either organized by the children themselves or by their elders seems to be woefully inadequate in our modern cities. In striking contrast to this, commercially controlled recreation seems to be growing by leaps and bounds. In the Newark Survey even at the early age of eight two-thirds of the boys were found to be going to the movies at least once a week. Groves (8) found that in a small town the school children spent an average of 13.8 cents a week on this form of amusement. It would probably be wrong to hold, as some extremists do, that all commercial recreation is a loss from the standpoint of the community. Yet Young (17) has estimated, after a careful study, that one-fifth of the films being shown to the American public are more or less objectionable from the moral standpoint. In any case, it would not be too much to say that attendance at the movies is a poor substitute for healthy, active, vigorous play activities.

What has been said about the movies would apply with even more force to dance halls, pool rooms, and amusement parks, some of which forms of commercial recreation bear a positively sinister reputation.

It would, of course, be distinctly unfortunate in any case if we had failed to provide for our children the opportunity for wholesome amusement, which is their right. However, if it can be shown that this failure of ours has had distinct moral implications and that the problem of juvenile delinquency is partly due to lack of adequate play, then the recreation problem immediately takes on a new and greatly enhanced seriousness. Careful scientific studies seem to prove that this is the case.

Perhaps the most interesting of these investigations is that of Thurston (14). The problem was to study a number of delinquent children and to determine, if possible, whether improper recreation or lack of recreation had any bearing on their delinquency. To get an unselected group, he took all the cases coming before the juvenile court in Cleveland in the first week of February, May, July, and October of one year. From these he eliminated some children who could not be located and some who were not primarily delinquency cases. He was left with a group of 95. To these were added 29 children who had not come before the court but who were suggested by branch librarians of the city as being notoriously badly behaved.

The results of Thurston's study were extremely interesting. In 94 out of his 124 cases, in other words, in more than three-fourths, he felt that there was "a clear connection" between delinquency and the spare time habits of the child.

This connection came about in various ways. Lack of wholesome opportunity for play led some of the children to spend their time around railroad yards and dumps, where they fell into minor delinquencies, such as stealing nuts and bolts and selling them for junk or stealing rides on freight trains. Other children had spent their time loafing about street corners or in parks. Here the old adage was verified that "the devil finds work for idle hands to do." Six boys loafing about a store learned that the owner was to be away all one day. They broke in and stole candies, cake, and tobacco. A group of girls idling about a park made the acquaintance of some young men of questionable character with unfortunate consequences.

Another type is represented by the boy who had just entered a business school. There he met a crowd of rather fast young men who enjoyed movies, burlesque shows, and club parties. He stole some money so as to be able to participate in these new forms of amusement. Sometimes the delinquency resulted from an attempt to keep up with the other members of a recreational group. A 13-year-old girl was arrested for stealing a shirt waist and skirt from a department store. She said that the girls laughed at her old-fashioned clothes and in order to qualify for admission into their circle she had considered it necessary to steal.

Some rather pathetic instances are furnished by the children whose delinquencies were an attempt to escape from a dull, monotonous life which did not have sufficient recreation. There was a little girl of 13 who had to care for no less than seven younger brothers and sisters. Her only opportunity for amusement came late at night when the other children were safe in bed and it brought her into contact with bad company.

A study by Gillin (6) should be compared with the above. Thurston studied delinquents to see whether their play habits had any connection with their delinquency, while Gillin studied a group of wholesome citizens to see whether their spare time habits had any connection with their wholesome citizenship. A group of men and women were picked as being representative of the better type of citizen. They were not necessarily rich or socially prominent, but all of them were characterized by wholesome lives and a commendable civic spirit.

All of these men and women were visited by

an investigator and their recreational lives from early childhood were minutely reviewed. The results would seem amply to prove the conclusion reached by Gillin—"We may conclude that the evidence shows that spare-time activities, either directly or indirectly, have had a vital influence upon the development of these people."

To compare Thurston's results with Gillin's seems to make a particularly effective argument for the need of recreation. The former showed delinquents were delinquents largely on account of their poor play habits, while the latter showed that wholesome citizens were wholesome citizens largely because of their constructive recreation.

Voelker (16) attacked the same problem in a very original way. Whereas other investigators had contented themselves with observation, Voelker decided to try a controlled experiment. He narrowed his problem down to one particular type of recreational work; namely, Scouting, and to one particular trait; namely, trustworthiness. He used several groups of children, some of whom had received Scout training and some of whom had not. He devised a test in which the children had an opportunity to prove whether or not they were trustworthy—whether they could be trusted, for example, to return to a shopkeeper extra change which he had given them through an arrangement with the investigator, or whether they could be trusted not to cheat in school when an opportunity was purposely given.

Voelker's first conclusion was that the group which had had Scout training showed a much higher average trustworthiness. But his most important results were based upon a comparison of four groups. All four were first tested and then, after the lapse of a period of time, a second series of tests was given. In the meantime, however, two of the groups, the experimental groups, received Scout training, while the other groups, the control groups, did not. It was found when the second series of tests had been administered that the experimental groups had improved immensely in trustworthiness as compared with the controls.

The results of the study mentioned above have been confirmed in large measure by practical experience. It has been stated that with the opening of playgrounds in South Chicago delinquency immediately fell off 29 per cent. The establishment of the Union League Boys' Clubs in the same city was said to have brought similarly striking results. Sullenger (13) found that

88 per cent of juvenile delinquents in Omaha lived more than a half a mile from the nearest playground.

Anyone who knows children will not be surprised at these results. Organized recreation obviously helps to prevent delinquency by "keeping the boys off the streets." On account of the fortunate difficulty of bilocation the lad who is attending a Scout meeting is not stealing rides on freight trains or breaking windows. And the girl who is playing tennis on a well-supervised playground is not picking up young men on the street corner.

But wholesome play has more important benefits than this merely negative one. At play the child is most nearly himself. He may listen passively to the moral instruction of his classroom teacher, but his real ideals are largely picked up at play. If his heroes on the baseball diamond are fine examples of American youth, then he, too, will be inspired to fine ideals. But if his play is on the streets and his heroes are picked from among street-corner loafers then, his ideals will be correspondingly debased.

Joseph Lee (10) has said that play is growth. The child who does not play is just to that degree queer, maladjusted, and abnormal. Such one-sided individuals are the stuff from which criminals are made. But the boy or girl who has experienced in play the give and take of citizenship, who has learned in his team games that the individual must sometimes sacrifice himself for the good of the group, is much more likely to become a good citizen. The battle of Waterloo may or may not have been won on the cricket fields of Eton, but the battles of the American democracy of the future are most certainly being fought in large measure upon the play areas where our children spend the vitally important hours of their leisure.

It is only with the present century that the movement to organize systematically the play of our children has reached large proportions. In part this is due to private initiative and in part to public appropriation and legislation. The privately-organized recreational movement has shown several distinct tendencies. Privately-organized clubs are sometimes large national bodies carefully centralized under a national headquarters or else they may consist of local clubs loosely bound together into a federation. It will be convenient to speak of the former as the *Scout-type* club and of the latter as the *federation type*.

The most conspicuous example of the Scout-type organization is furnished naturally by the

Boy Scouts of America. This enormous body can well boast of being the largest boys' club in the world, since its present membership approximates two-thirds of a million. The Boy Scouts derive their importance not only from their size but from the fact that they have been the first and the most widely imitated organization of this type.

One man, Sir Robert Baden-Powell, is responsible for this movement. As early as 1893, being at that time an English army officer, he began to experiment with some novel methods of military training which emphasized self-reliance and the competitive spirit. Five years later he published *Aids to Scouting,* which described many of these novel methods. Various people in England recognized the value of his ideas as a recreational program and *Scouting,* as the new movement was called, grew rapidly, until, in 1910, Baden-Powell gave up his commission in the army to devote his full time to it.

In 1910, also, Scouting was introduced into America by Mr. W. D. Boyce, who had been favorably impressed by it during a visit to England. Since that time it has grown both in this country and abroad rapidly and constantly. Scouting, in America, is characterized by an extremely centralized overhead organization. The

National Council, which meets annually, controls the movement through a national headquarters in New York. Every boy who joins must be registered at national headquarters. Every *Troop,* as the local units are called, must receive its charter and each official, both paid and volunteer, must get his commission from the same source. The tests by which boys advance to higher ranks of Scouting are prescribed also by the national authorities.

There are at least two other salient characteristics which distinguish Scouting sharply from other national organizations. One is its refusal to invest in buildings. The Troops are supported by churches, schools, playgrounds, clubs, and similar agencies, and meet in rooms furnished by them. The Scouts themselves own almost no buildings. The other characteristic of the Scouts is their reliance on volunteer leadership. Every Troop is in charge of a Scoutmaster who is a volunteer, and the paid men, the executives, do not, in general, take active charge of the actual work with boys, but confine themselves to such administrative activities as the organization of Troops, publicity work, and the training of volunteer leaders.

The Scouts have served as a model for a large number of other national bodies. The Girl

Scouts, Camp Fire Girls, the Boy Rangers, the Catholic Boys' Brigade, the Pioneer Youth of America, and numerous other movements show the general outlines characteristic of Scouting— a national headquarters, a nationally approved series of tests, the passing of which allows the members to pass from lower to higher ranks, a reliance upon volunteer leadership, and a refusal to invest in buildings.

The federation-type of national organization shows distinct differences from the Scout type. The latter's national headquarters becomes the final source of authority, while the federation-type organization consists of a number of individual clubs bound together more or less loosely into a national body. The Boys' Club Federation is an example of this. It consists of a large number of boys' clubs organized in various cities throughout the country. Nearly all of these clubs own their own club houses and employ paid directors. The Federation is merely a voluntary union of these various clubs. It prescribes no program and exercises no control at all over the member clubs except the informal control of good advice. In contrast to the Scouts, it depends principally upon paid leadership, and volunteers play only a very subordinate part.

The Y. M. C. A. is an old organization which

again is only loosely centralized. The national
body merely suggests programs and methods and
the individual clubs choose what they wish from
these. It has no machinery for keeping its member clubs in line and it relies only on its *esprit
de corps* to secure uniformity throughout the
nation.

Camping must be mentioned here as another
example of a national movement developing
principally under private auspices. The date of
the first camp is generally given as 1881, at
which time Mr. Ernest Balch established a boys'
camp on Chocorua Island. Although the organized camp thus has a relatively long history, it
is only within the last few years that it has had
its most rapid development. Exact statistics on
the size of the movement are lacking. But a survey made by the Playground and Recreation
Association of America in 1923 estimated that
even at that time between eight hundred thousand and one million persons spent some time
in camp in the United States every year.

The recent history of the camping movement
has been characterized by at least two striking
developments. The first of these has been the
tendency for regulation and standardization.
This has been partly through surveys and the
consequent adoption of voluntary standards and

partly it has been through legislative regulation. At the present time about three-fourths of the states have some form of state regulation of camping.

The other tendency has been the growth of the low-priced camp. The early camps were generally privately managed and catered to the class which could afford to pay a large fee. The private camp is still increasing in popularity but its growth has never equaled the immense strides which the low-priced camps have been making. The latter type generally charges from seven to ten dollars a week and is managed by some church, club, or other organization which is able to bear at least part of the expense. Another interesting recent development, particularly in the United States. has been the organization of municipal camps in which the city provides camping facilities for its citizens at a reasonable rate.

The playground also developed as a private recreational movement at first. The early playgrounds were looked on as charities and were designed primarily for the children of the poor. The decade between 1890 and 1900 was the charity era in the history of the movement. It soon began to be realized, however, that the playground was too important an element in civic life to be abandoned to the somewhat haphazard support of private individuals or societies. With the turn of the century the municipal playground began to be important. These early playgrounds were generally administered by the park department. Somewhere around 1910 the movement had grown to such an extent that separate city departments, often called *recreation departments,* were organized to take care of playgrounds, bathing beaches, and other recreational projects supported by the city. This still represents the best practice in municipal recreation.

Many people feel that at least as far as the school child is concerned, the school department will have to assume in the future the direction of the child's recreation. The interest of educators in play goes back through the physical education movement at least to the middle of the last century. But the spirit behind physical education was not favorable to the development of the play spirit. Men like Jahn looked upon physical education as a method of developing healthy bodies for the service of the state. Consequently educators in this country, when they began to interest themselves in physical education, generally confined their work to formal drill with a minimum of the play spirit.

The last decade or so has seen the growth of what is often called the *newer physical education*. Leaders have realized first that no system of formal drill can give quite the same all-round development to all the muscles of the body as can healthy, normal, play. Secondly, as we have begun to realize, play itself has a value simply as play and that to deprive the children's activities of their spontaneity, as had been done in the old formal drill, was to deprive these activities of one of their most important values.

The newer physical education therefore represents the confluence of two important movements—the play movement, which emphasized the importance of play in the development of character, and the older physical-educational movement, which recognized the school's responsibility toward the bodies as well as the minds of the children. Many feel that the school of the future will have a long day, including play periods of at least two hours a day, and that an effort will be made, even outside of school time, to make the school the headquarters of the child's play activities (11). This wider concept of the school's responsibility to the community is shown also by the rapid growth of *evening centers* or *community centers* in the school buildings (7).

Whatever may be the details we may be sure that in the future the community will make a very decided and conscious effort to provide for all its citizens, particularly for the young, an opportunity to have plenty of recreation of a type which shall be at once worth while in the eyes of the child and in the eyes of the community. What proportion of this shall be controlled by the public authorities and what proportion by private persons is as yet an undecided question. There remain also such details as the relative advantages of the Scout-type of club and the federation-type, and the question of the degree to which publicly supported recreation ought to be centralized in the school. One point, however, is clear: America is awakening to the importance of recreation as a child-welfare problem and will not rest content until that problem is satisfactorily solved.

## BIBLIOGRAPHY

(1) Baden-Powell, Sir Robert: *Scouting for boys, a handbook for instruction in good citizenship.* Tenth edition. London, C. Arthur Pearson, Ltd., 1922. 338 p.
The English handbook for Scouts.

(2) Bonser, Frederick Gordon: *School work and spare time.* Cleveland, O., The Survey Committee of the Cleveland Foundation, 1918. 176 p.
A study of the play of Cleveland children.

(3)  Boy Scouts of America: *Community boy leadership;
     a manual for Scout Executives.* Second edition.
     New York, Pub. under the supervision of the
     Editorial Board representing the National Council
     of the Boy Scouts of America, 1922.  622 p.
     A handbook for Scout Executives.

(4)  Boy Scouts of America: *Handbook for Scoutmasters;
     a manual of leadership.* Second handboook, fifth
     imprint.  New York, Pub. under the supervision
     of the Editorial Board representing the National
     Council of the Boy Scouts of America, 1923.
     632 p.
     Advice for Scoutmasters.  The psychology is anti-
     quated.

(5)  Boy Scouts of America: *Revised handbook for boys.*
     First Edition, New York, Boy Scouts of America,
     1927.  638 p.
     An entire revision of this important book.

(6)  Gillin, John Lewis: *Wholesome citizens and spare
     time.*  Cleveland, O., The Survey Committee of
     the Cleveland Foundation, 1918.  182 p.
     The effect of play on wholesome citizenship.

(7)  Glueck, *Mrs.* Eleanor (Touroff); *The community
     use of schools.*  Baltimore, The Williams & Wil-
     kins Company, 1927.  xiv, 222 p.
     A standard work on the subject.

(8)  Groves, J. W.: "Elementary school children and the
     movies."  *Sch. and Soc.*, 18:659-60, December 1,
     1923.
     A study of a group in a small town.

(9)  Johnson, George Ellsworth: *Education through
     recreation.*  Cleveland, O., The Survey Commit-
     tee of the Cleveland Foundation, 1916.  94 p.

The play of the school child from the educator's standpoint.

(10) Lee, Joseph: *Play in education.* New York, The Macmillan Company, 1915. xxiii, 500 p.
A fascinating, though unscientific, interpretation of childhood and play.

(11) Nash, Jay B.: *The organization and administration of playgrounds and recreation.* New York, A. S. Barnes & Company, 1927. xii, 547 p.
Probably the best book on municipally controlled recreation.

(12) Newark, N. J. Rotary Club, Boys' Work Committee: *Survey of the boys of Newark, New Jersey.* Newark, N. J. Boys' Work Committee of the Newark Rotary Club, n. d. 89 p.
One of the best modern surveys.

(13) Sullenger, T. Earl: *A summary of a study of the juvenile delinquent in Omaha.* Omaha, Nebraska, University of Omaha, 1925. 17 p. incl. covertitle. (University of Omaha Bulletin, Vol 1, No. 3.)
Includes a study of recreation.

(14) Thurston, Henry W.: *Delinquency and spare time; a study of a few stories written into the court records of the city of Cleveland.* Cleveland, O., The Survey Committee of the Cleveland Foundation, 1918. 189 p.
A carefully controlled study of the effect of recreation on delinquency.

(15) U. S. Bureau of Education: *A manual of educational legislation for the guidance of committees on education of the state legislatures.* Washington, D. C., U. S. Gov't Printing Office, 1925. iii, 51

p.   (U. S. Bureau of Education Bull. No. 36, 1924.)
Includes figures on school attendance.

(16) Voelker, Paul Frederick: *The function of ideals and attitudes in social education, an experimental study.* New York, Teachers College, Columbia University, 1921. v, 126 p.   (Teachers College Contributions to Education No. 112.)
An account of an interesting experiment on the effect of Scouting.

(17) Young, Donald Ramsey: *Motion pictures; a study in social legislation.* Philadelphia, Westbrook Publishing Co., 1922. 109 p. Ph. D. thesis, University of Pennsylvania.)
Believes 20 per cent of movies have some demoralizing effect.

# CHAPTER IX

## *The Child and His Job*

There can be no doubt that vocational malad-justment is responsible for a great economic loss. When the boy who would make an excellent bricklayer becomes a poor lawyer and when the girl who would make an excellent teacher becomes a mediocre shop-girl the resulting loss of efficiency is quite evident. What is even more serious is the effect on the maladjusted individuals themselves. Unless a job is hard enough to call out the worker's full powers as well as easy enough to be performed by him with a measure of success he will not be entirely happy. On the other hand the worker who finds his labor interesting will be likely to be a contented person. The ranks of the lawless are largely recruited from those who have no jobs or who find their jobs uninteresting.

There can be little doubt that such vocational maladjustment is considerable. Edgerton (7) reports a study of the occupational choices of several thousand secondary school pupils. Thirty-five and nine-tenths per cent of them had chosen one of the professions as their life work. Since only about five per cent of the general population belong in this class it appears that many of these pupils are doomed to be disappointed. Feingold (8) reports that among a group of high school students only 46 per cent chose vocations within their range of intelligence. Forty-seven per cent chose vocations above their mental level and seven per cent chose vocations which were too low. If the choice of vocations is made thus unintelligently there can be little doubt that the preparation for it is also rather haphazard. Snedden (15) estimates that out of sixty million adult workers employed either gainfully or as homemakers fully fifty million have received their training by mere "pick-up" methods.

In view of these facts it appears that our children have been left in the past to pick their life work and to prepare for it largely by mere chance methods, with a resulting appalling waste of human happiness, as well as of money. The aim of the vocational guidance movement is to give the children in our schools the information and counsel which will help them to choose their life work intelligently and to prepare themselves for it in the most efficient manner.

Before the school can advise intelligently it must itself be in possession of a reliable body of vocational information. Much of this can be assembled from published sources, such as the reports of the United States Census Bureau, special investigating commissions, or research bureaus. A great deal of this material is available in convenient handbooks, many of which have been published with the growth of the vocational guidance movement.

Vocational information of this general character can be adapted to many of the local occupations. Certain positions, such as that of physician, bookkeeper, or stenographer vary only slightly from one part of the country to another. Published studies of these occupations, therefore, can usually be made to fit the local situation. There are often other jobs, however, which are more or less peculiar to the locality. In such cases it will be necessary to make original studies of these occupations together with their requirements and opportunities in order to be in a position to advise intelligently. A study of the work permits granted by the city during the last few years will usually suggest some of the occupations which are most important from the standpoint of the young worker, but this must be supplemented by other studies.

There is a wide divergency of practice in making these occupational studies. Sometimes they are made by counselors from the school and sometimes by placement workers. The feeling seems to be growing, however, that such studies require so much skill and training in research that they should be made by specialists. Sometimes a city employs a staff of visiting experts to makes these studies when its vocational guidance program is inaugurated. A better arrangement still, where the city can afford it, is to employ one or more specialists permanently attached to the vocational guidance bureau who spend their full time in making these studies and in bringing the old ones up to date.

The essential points to be covered in such a study include a brief description of the occupation and its importance, the age and sex of the workers, the names and locations of the local shops, rates of wages, and the demand for new workers. The study should further specify the amount and sort of preparation needed and the opportunities for acquiring this preparation either in the industry itself, in the local schools, or otherwise. The study should bring out the advantages and disadvantages of the job so that the boys and girls in the school may make up their minds intelligently in regard to it.

When this information has been assembled in convenient form the next task is to make it available to the pupils. This is accomplished in various ways in different localities. Some cities print and distribute pamphlets. Some use posters on the school bulletin boards. Again, outside specialists may be called in to address school assemblies about training in particular occupations. Extra-curricular activities may also be made to play their part. The students who interest themselves in the school paper will readily acquire some knowledge of opportunities in journalism. Members of orchestras or glee clubs willl learn something about the possibilities of music as a career. Members of clubs devoted to photography, radio, or other special subjects may be taught something about the opportunities open in these different lines.

One of the most efficient ways of presenting this information, however, is by organizing special life-career classes in the junior high schools for the express purpose of imparting vocational information. These classes are usually taught by the local counselors, who thus have the opportunity of getting acquainted with the children in class as well as by interviews outside of class.

The subject matter of such a class falls under two heads. The general principles underlying the choice of a career are first emphasized. Then specific occupations are studied and the information which has been gathered from general sources or from local studies is imparted to the pupils.

The above methods of giving vocational information are efficient. They have, however, the one fault that they are apt to be a bit theoretical. A boy may listen all day to the advantages and disadvantages of drafting as a career but he will probably be better able to decide whether he will like this job or not if he is given a drawing board and a set of drafting tools and is taught some of the elementary principles of the work.

With this idea in mind many of our progressive school systems offer some pre-vocational or exploratory courses. These are short courses in different subjects, generally of a practical nature, which are offered to the pupils to help them to choose their vocation in life and the necessary courses to prepare for it. Such classes are particularly common in the junior high school. Opportunities for tryouts in industrial subjects are furnished by courses in electrical work, printing, automobile repairing, wood, and metal work, and in similar subjects. Classes in "business practice" offer exploratory work in the commercial field. The traditional academic subjects are themselves a fairly satisfactory exploratory course in professional and academic training.

Prevocational courses must not be confused with genuine vocational training. The difference between the two lies in the fact that the former should precede the choice of a vocation while the latter should follow it. The exploratory courses are characteristically short and a bit sketchy. They offer little real training for actual work in the occupation. On the other hand genuine vocational courses aim to fit the pupil at least to make a beginning at earning a livelihood.

To give the pupil a maximum of help in choosing his vocation it is not enough to give him occupational information as a member of a group. Each pupil is a separate problem. To meet this problem the information ought to be adapted to each particular case. This information, together with information about school courses is often made available to the child by the school counselor. His function is to help the individual child to make his individual adjustment.

The duties of counselors vary a great deal in different cities. At one extreme we find the term applied to a classroom teacher whose counseling activities include little more than the giving of advice which any intelligent teacher might be expected to give to her pupils. At the other we find specially trained counselors who give their entire time to counseling and do no teaching at all except possibly to give a course in vocational information. Where the latter type of organization is found the counselors may either be attached to some central bureau of vocational guidance or to individual schools or else some combination of these two plans may be used.

Most school systems which have a counseling program try to make it available to all the pupils. This is an ideal, however, which is seldom attained in practice on account of the lack of facilities. Usually only those pupils are reached who show a very special need for vocational counsel. These include pupils who are making out curricular programs, those who have chosen courses for which they are obviously unfit, and those who are in danger of dropping out of school or who have actually left.

The success of vocational counsel depends upon the extent to which it meets the needs of the individual. Therefore the better the coun-

selor knows each case with which he has to deal
the better advice he will be able to give. The
sources of this information are various. The
school record will give the counselor some insight into the childs' intelligence and his ability
to stick at a task and bring it to a successful conclusion. Reports from visiting teachers and social
agencies will present a picture of the home background. Many school systems use systematic
questionnaires which the child fills out some
time during his junior high school course. More
important than any of these courses is the personal interview. By this means the sympathetic
counselor can get an insight into the child's personality which the more impersonal sources
mentioned above would fail to give.

Mental tests are becoming more and widely
used as an aid in guidance work. Many progressive school systems attempt to give some group
tests to all their pupils. These are supplemented
by individual examinations in doubtful cases.
The school record may include the results of
some standardized achievement tests in the ordinary school subjects. The results of all these
should be available to the counselor. Not only
will they aid him in advising the child to avoid
courses too difficult for him but they will give
a considerable amount of help in the choice of

a vocation. Recent research has shown that the choice of a vocation is limited by intelligence. The boy with an IQ of 80 will not make an efficient bookkeeper. The girl with an IQ of 130 would probably find the duties of a shopgirl uninteresting. Intelligence tests do not indicate what specific occupations would best suit the subject but they do reveal the general range of occupations within which he will be most at home.

Recent research by Hull (11) and others has suggested the possibility of determining an individual's aptitude more closely than can be done by the ordinary intelligence tests. The newer type of vocational tests will possibly be able to determine which of two boys of similar intelligence would make the better physician and which the better engineer. Much further research will be necessary, however, before tests of this kind will be used widely in actual guidance work.

The newer type of school has definitely accepted the responsibility of helping the child to choose his vocation. It also gives him a certain amount of the necessary training. It would be illogical not to take the third step and find the job as well. It is not surprising, therefore, to find that many cities have organized a placement service for juniors. The process of vocational guidance thus becomes a continuous one beginning with the giving of vocational information in the grades and in ending only when the child has been placed in a position adapted to his ability.

The placement bureau is usually organized under the school system as a part of the vocational guidance work. In some places this office has been placed under some other department but the advantages of a close connection with the school system are obvious. With whatever department the bureau is connected an effort should be made to tie up the placement work closely with it.

An essential task of the placement service is to secure a list of available positions. There is no easy way to do this. The office can hope to build up a list of clients among business organizations only by giving continuous satisfaction in its everyday work. Business firms may be interested in the functions of the placement bureau by means of talks given before service clubs or other business organizations. In large cities such as New York, Philadelphia, or Chicago a district plan is usually employed in accordance with which one worker is made responsible for soliciting jobs from firms in a particular part of the city.

As in vocational counsel so also in junior placement the success of the work depends very largely on the close study of the individual case. It is only when such knowledge is available that the placement worker can select the right child for the right job. This information should become available by a close coöperation with the school system which should have accumulated it in the course of its guidance work. It is thus possible to form a more intelligent estimate of the abilities and personality of the applicant. Unfortunately the practice of many cities has fallen below this standard. The school has had a rather comprehensive knowledge of the child and then, through lack of coördination, has failed to make this knowledge available to the placement office. Consequently the latter institution has depended largely on a single interview to gather its knowledge of the applicant.

The placement office should be located at some place readily accessible to the applicants and at the same time near the principal centers of employment. The arrangement of the office itself is also important. The ideal plan is to have a number of small separate rooms so that the placement worker may enjoy a certain degree of privacy when interviewing the applicant.

When the applicant comes to the office the first thing to do is to assemble all available information concerning him. Sometimes a clerk is assigned to the task of meeting all applicants and arranging the order of their interviews. In this case she will collect the information from the files and put it on the desk of the placement counselor before the applicant enters. Many offices obtain this information with a questionnaire either filled out by the applicant himself while he is waiting or by the placement counselor during the interview. In any case the interview itself forms an important part of the procedure. By it the worker is enabled to get a more accurate impression of the applicant's personality than the records alone would have given.

Sometimes a position may be found among those already on file. If this fails the office usually undertakes solicitation by telephone. When a position is found the applicant is generally given a card which will introduce him to the prospective employer. The placement counselor instructs him how to reach the place of employment and what will be expected of him. The employer is generally asked to sign the application card and return it to the office in case the applicant is accepted. The office is thus informed that the position is filled and is enabled to close its records. If the card is not returned the employer is generally called by telephone to find what action has been taken.

The work of the placement office does not stop as soon as the position has been filled. Some system of follow-up should be used so that the office may keep in touch with the junior worker until it has assured itself that both the employer and employe are satisfied. There are two principal ways of accomplishing this. Either the employer may be visited and interviewed or the junior worker may be encouraged to come back and discuss his job with the placement counselor. Some offices send out form letters inviting the junior worker to visit the placement office and for this reason evening office hours are held.

A special problem facing placement workers is the "blind-alley" job. There is considerable diversity of opinion here. Some feel that only such positions should be secured for applicants as offer a definite hope for future advancement. Others admit that this is the ideal condition yet feel that it is impossible to secure enough desirable positions for all applicants. They feel that the blind-alley job is often the only position available for the young boy or girl seeking employment. They contend that if an efficient system of follow-up is in force it will be possible to guide these workers into more promising positions as soon as they are mature enough to fill them.

There is another system of vocational adjustment perhaps even more effective than the work of the placement office—the combination of school and employment. Sometimes this takes the form of "coöperative courses." In these the pupils may spend half a day in school and half a day at work or else they may work and go to school during alternate weeks, two pupils occupying the same position by turns. Such courses may be organized in special trade schools or in the high schools. Instruction given under these conditions is likely to appear more actual to the child than it would if all his time were spent at school. Unfortunately practical difficulties have made these coöperative courses rather rare. But they offer interesting possibilities.

A variant of this is the "apprenticeship course" such as has been tried for example in Chicago and Boston. This implies an agreement between the school and the trade-union authorities in accordance with which the theoretical part of the union's program of apprenticeship training is given by the school.

Another form of coördination between the school and the job is represented by the "continuation school." This is a school attended by employed minors for a few hours each week. Although the principal reason for such classes is, of course, to keep the school in touch with the child as long as possible, they do offer some opportunity for educational tie-up and further counseling. All the above systems have the common merit that they make the transition from school to work more gradual and that they bring employers and school authorities into a helpful and coöperative relationship.

The concept of the school's function outlined in this chapter differs strikingly from the traditional one. Old-fashioned educators shaped their curricula with a view to college entrance. They felt that any compromise with "practical" aims was somehow beneath the dignity of an institution of learning and that any child who dropped out of their schools was an educational tragedy. The newer school has a much broader view of education. It feels that its function is to fit the child for life whether this implies instruction in algebra or pattern making, in Xenophon or domestic science. If the child appears to be promising material for higher education the school stands ready to fit him for it. But if he is prevented by economic reasons or mental limitation from entering college, the school is no less anxious to help to fit him for some other career. In either case the child is being educated —fitted for life—and in either case the school accepts the responsibility for his education.

## BIBLIOGRAPHY

(1) Allen, Frederick James: *Practice in vocational guidance; a book of readings*. New York, etc., Mc-Graw-Hill Book Company, Inc., 1927. ix, 306 p.
A book of brief readings by authorities in the field.

(2) Allen, Frederick James: *Principles and problems in vocational guidance; a book of readings*. New York, etc., McGraw-Hill Book Company, Inc., 1927. ix, 390 p.
A companion volume to the above.

(3) Brewer, John Marks, Blake, Mabelle B., Bresnehen, Ella L., and others: *Case studies in educational and vocational guidance*. Boston, New York, etc., Ginn and Company. 1926. xxiv, 243 p.
An excellentt work.

(4) Brewer, John Marks, Blake, Mabelle B., Douglass, L. C., and others: *Mental measurements in educational and vocational guidance; a condensed statement of the problem, the means available, the appropriate procedure, and the results achieved*. Cambridge, Mass., Harvard University, 1924. vi, 46 p.
A brief treatment of the uses of tests in guidance.

(5) Burtt, Harold Ernest: *Principles of employment psychology.* Boston, New York, etc., Houghton Mifflin Company, 1926. xi, 568 p.
An outstanding treatment of the contribution of psychology to the employer.

(6) Edgerton, A. H., and Cunliffe, R. B.: "A public school program for collecting and using occupational information." *23rd Yearbook, N. S. S. E., Part II*, 119-38. 1924.
Shows how local occupational surveys may be made.

(7) Edgerton, A. H.: *Vocational guidance and counseling, including reports on preparation of school Conselors.* New York, The Macmillian Company, 1926. xvii, 213 p.
Valuable especially as indicating the preliminary training necessary for successful counseling.

(8) Feingold, G. A.: "The relation between the intelligence and vocational choices of high school pupils." *Jr. Apl. Psychol.*, 7:143-53, June, 1923.
Little relation is found.

(9) Franklin, Edward Earle: *The permanence of the vocational interests of junior high school pupils.* Baltimore, Johns Hopkins University Press, 1924. vii, 64 p. (The Johns Hopkins University Studies in Education No. 8.)
Interests found to be very changeable.

(10) Fryer, Douglas: "The significance of interest for vocational prognosis." *Mental Hygiene*, 8:466-505, 1924.
Vocational ambition is a nearly worthless index of aptitude.

(11) Hull, Clark L.: *Aptitude testing.* Yonkers-on-Hudson, New York, aand Chicago, Illinois, World Book Company, 1928. xiv, 535 p.
The best reference on the new "aptitude tests."

(12) Kitson, Harry Dexter: *The psychology of vocational adjustment.* Philadelphia, Chicago, etc. J. B. Lippincott Company, 1925. viii, 273 p.
An excellent work on the subject.

(13) Lane, May Rogers: *Occupational studies, survey of their uses, content, and volume, and bibliography, history, and reviews of research-pamphlet series* 1920-1926. Scranton, Pa., International Textbook Company, 1927. 81 p.
Good Bibliography

(14) Limp, Chas. E.: "The use of the regression equation in determining the aptitudes of an individual." *Jr. Ed. Psychol.*, 16:414-18, September, 1925.
An attempt to distinguish aptitudes in English and typewriting by a number of tests.

(15) Snedden, David: "Vocational education in the United States; principles and issues." *Sch. and Soc.*, 25:292-95, March 5, 1927.
A brief review of the fundamental facts.

(16) Strong, Edward K.: "Differentiation of certified public accountants from other occupational groups." *Jr. Ed. Psychol.,* 18:227-38, April, 1927
An example of the new technique of discovering vocational aptitudes by test batteries.

(17) U. S. Children's Bureau: *Vocational guidance and junior placement; twelve cities in the United States.* Prepared by the Industrial Division of the Children's Bureau and the Junior Division of the United States Employment Service. Washington,

D. C., U. S. Gov't Printing Office, 1925.   xii,
440 p.   (Children's Bureau Publication No. 149.)
Perhaps the best single reference on the whole
field.   It is based on intensive studies made in 12
cities.

# CHAPTER X

## Child Labor

According to the federal census of 1920 there were in this country somewhat more than a million children between 10 and 16 years old "engaged in gainful occupations." This represented about a twelfth of the total population of this age. Of these children 378,663 were under 14. Although these figures were large enough to be striking they probably understated the case. For they did not include children doing household tasks or irregular work around the home farm. Furthermore they failed to take account of working children under ten whose number is known to be considerable. Since the census was taken in January it did not inculde vacation workers. Finally the child-labor situation at the time of the census was probably not typical because of the Second Federal Child-Labor Law which was then in effect but has since been declared unconstitutional.

It is scarcely necessary to enlarge upon the evil

217

effects which result from child labor. The mere fact that the child must have his education cut short in order to go to work is very unfortunate. Add to this the physical effect of labor on the growing organism, the unwholesome moral effects which often follow from the working environment, and the psychological effect of being deprived of a normal, happy childhood and it becomes clear that child labor is a crime against the rising generation. The right to play and to unhampered self-development must be assured to every child. The greed of selfish employers must be curbed. Where parents are impelled by economic stress to send their young children to work the remedy is to be sought not in laxer child-labor laws but in general economic reform which shall assure every family an income sufficient for a reasonable standard of living without exploiting the labor of the young child.

The employment of children is not subject to the flagrant abuses of 30 or 40 years ago; but it is still a grave problem as may be seen from the figures quoted above. There is considerable room for improvement both in the laws themselves and in their enforcement. It would be distinctly a mistake, therefore, to believe that there is no longer any need for concern in regard to the problem of child labor.

It is very hard to make sweeping statements about the present child-labor laws because they vary so much between state and state, and admit of so many exceptions. However, certain standards are fairly well recognized throughout the country and all states have at least made a good beginning in the regulation of child labor.

All the states of the Union except Wyoming and Utah have a minimum age below which certain forms of employment are forbidden. In seven states this minimum age is 15 or over. But so many exceptions are allowed by law that the effect of the provision is very much impaired. Most states have also a minimum educational requirement. In some states the completion of eight grades is demanded; but 18 states either have no educational requirement at all or else require only ability to read and write or do elementary arithmetic. All except 15 states require children to submit to a physical examination at least in some cases, but only 25 states make such an examination mandatory. Besides the general minimum age there is often a special requirement for work at certain hazardous occupations. For instance, most of the important mining states require a child to be 16 or even older before he may work in the mines.

Thirty-eight states and the District of Columbia have an eight-hour day for at least some children but nine, including several important industrial states, permit children under sixteen to work nine hours or more a day. Most states which have an eight-hour day also have a forty-eight-hour week. Another common requirement affecting hours of labor is the prohibition of night work for children under a certain age.

Besides the child-labor laws themselves compulsory school-attendance laws indirectly affect employment of children. All states have such legislation in some form. Six require attendance up to 14 or 15; 28 require it up to 16, while 14 states insist on school attendance to the age of 17 or 18 years at least in some localities. This legislation, however, is weakened by very numerous exceptions. For instance, it is a frequent rule that children from 14 to 16 may be allowed to work if they have completed certain educational requirements (18).

The foregoing laws affect children under 16, but there is also a child-labor problem which concerns children between 16 and 18. According to the census of 1920 there were 221,298 girls and 366,215 boys of this age employed in factories alone. Laws applying to this age group generally prohibit certain specified dangerous or morally hazardous occupations and regulate hours of labor and night work. As has been said already, 14 states require school attendance for at least certain children of this age (10).

It may be seen from the above that child-labor legislation is in a fairly satisfactory condition in this country. It still leaves, however, something to be desired. The laws are often weakened by numerous exceptions and they are not always adequately enforced.

This is true even in the case of child labor in factories which was the first abuse to be attacked by legislation. When the First Federal Child-Labor Law was in force government inspectors visited 689 mills and factories finding 385 children under the age of 14 at work, as well as 978 between 14 and 16 working more than eight hours a day (15). A study of the oyster and shrimp canning communities on the Gulf Coast (12) showed that 106 out of 542 child workers between six and fifteen had never attended school. Of all the children studied 41 per cent were not attending school when the survey was made. Of 544 children 334 were under 14. Many of these were children of migratory workers living amid wretched conditions in company shacks. Two hundred and seventy-eight of the children were below the legal working age of the state in which they were employed. Federal inspections made in 1922 in the textile mills of Georgia (22) found that the state law had been violated in 149 instances in 39 mills.

Industrial work at home can be very much abused. A study of three communities in Rhode Island (20) showed that about eight per cent of the school children between the ages of five and fifteen did some work at home. Almost one-half of these were under 11 years of age and 86 per cent were under 14. A more recent study in New Jersey (13) revealed that 63 per cent of the home workers included in the study were children under 16 years of age and 27 per cent were mothers. Almost a quarter of the children were under 10. Even during school time the majority of the children worked two or three hours a day. Industrial work at home, therefore, is a serious problem. It should certainly be regulated by good legislation while the economic stress which induces families to take up home work should be relieved by general welfare measures.

A great weakness in many state laws is their failure to regulate child labor on farms. Although a few states have made a beginning in such legislation, it is still largely an unsolved problem. Public indifference to this question has probably been due to the feeling that farm work is a healthy, outdoor occupation and that it is good for the child. While it is doubtless true that a certain amount of such work is beneficial the conditions revealed by studies of child labor on farms have been deplorable.

A study by the Children's Bureau of the child labor on Maryland truck farms (5) showed that nine-tenths of the children under 16 enrolled in the schools in the districts studied had worked on the farms during the preceding year. About one-half of the boys reported having worked nine hours or more on the last working day preceding the study. It was not at all unusual to find negro girls working nine or ten hours a day.

In North Dakota (17) another study showed that boys of eight and girls of ten worked with heavy farm implements, plows, cultivators, and mowers. More than one sixth of the potato pickers were children under ten. Conditions in Illinois (25) were somewhat similar. Two-thirds of the boys and almost one-fifth of the girls in the schools studied had worked in the fields. Of the child workers 38 per cent were under 12 and 14 per cent were under ten. In the tobacco growing areas of Kentucky, South Carolina, Virginia, and the Connecticut Valley, a great deal of the work was done by children (3). In the southern states included in this study about one-half of the employed children were under twelve and one-fifth were under ten. One-fourth of the child workers in Connecticut, one-third in South Carolina and Virginia, and two-fifths in Kentucky, worked ten or more hours a day. A similar picture is presented by the cotton growing areas of Texas (23). Nearly all the children over ten included in this study had worked in the fields. Of the white children under ten years old 42 per cent, and of those under eight years old 26 per cent, had been employed. Conditions among negro children were even worse.

A particularly acute problem is furnished by the migratory child workers. In many parts of the country whole families "follow the crops," that is, they take up residence in a farming district during the harvest season to get temporary work. Since the harvesting of perishable crops must be done quickly we find children working from dawn almost to sunset and living in overcrowded labor camps under most unsanitary conditions. Since these children move from place to place school attendance laws are particularly difficult to enforce.

Among children of migratory families working in the fruit and hop growing districts of the northern Pacific Coast (4) 34 per cent of the workers were under 12 and 12 per cent were

under ten. Forty-three per cent of the children
working in the Willamette and Yakima Vallies
worked ten hours a day or more. In the sugar
beet farms of certain districts of the South Platte
Valley (1) a study of the farms which employed
child labor revealed that about one-half of the
workers were under 16 and about one-tenth
under ten. During the harvest season when
schools were in session one-fourth of the children worked an average of 11 hours and 13
minutes a day. This includes both local and
migratory workers. About one-half of the migratory workers on truck and small-fruit farms in
New Jersey were under 12 and one-fifth were
under 10. Over 40 per cent of these children
worked more than eight hours a day (24).

It may be concluded from the above studies
and from other similar ones that a great deal remains to be done before the child-labor problem
will be completely solved. Many have felt that
this will be best accomplished by a federal law.
Two attempts to regulate the employment of
children by federal legislation have failed. The
First Federal Child-Labor Law was passed
September 1, 1916 and became effective one year
later. It prohibited the interstate transportation
of goods made in factories where children under
14 were employed or where children under 16

worked more than eight hours a day, six days a week, or at night. It also banned the products of mines or quarries employing any children under 16. The Supreme Court declared this law unconstitutional on June 3, 1918.

A second law was included in the Revenue Act of September 24, 1916 and placed a heavy tax on all employers who violated the above standards. This also was declared unconstitutional on May 15, 1922. In 1924 Congress passed a constitutional amendment which would give the Federal Government power to regulate the employment of children under 18. This has aroused considerable opposition among those who believe that it would encroach on the rights of the states. At the present writing only five states have ratified it. Whether or not a constitutional amendment represents the wisest answer to the problem of child labor, few humane persons would fail to agree with the very conservative standard proposed by the first and second federal laws. In spite of this fact almost two-thirds of existing state laws fail to measure up to even this standard in every respect.

As important perhaps as legislation is the creation of an intelligent public opinion in favor of good child-labor standards. This makes necessary educational work. The two outstanding agencies at present active in this work are the United States Children's Bureau and the National Child Labor Committee. Both of these bodies have made studies, distributed literature, and assisted in the formulation of standards.

The enforcement of child-labor laws is equally important with the passage of the laws themselves as the studies quoted above indicate. Woodbury (26) summarizes the experience of Children's Bureau investigators who studied the enforcement of the child-labor laws in a number of states and cities. From this study it is apparent that the secret of successful enforcement is an efficient system of employment certificates. Such certificates should be required for all occupations at all ages at which child labor is subject to regulation. The minimum age for the certificate will be, therefore, the same as the minimum age for legal employment during school hours.

The best and most common employment certificate system involves local issuing officers under the supervision of a state agency. The local officers are most commonly school officials whereas the state supervising agency is most freqently connected with the state labor department. It might seem that this arrangement which combines two separate sorts of officials; namely, those from the local schools and those from some state industrial agency, might cause friction. In practice, however, it seems to work out well. Whoever the local officials are they ought to be properly trained, free from political influence, and paid a salary. The last requirement seems obvious enough, yet in actual fact some officials are still paid on the fee system. The law should be so worded that it should not be within the competency of the issuing officers to set aside the standards in particular cases.

State supervision may take various forms. The state agency should furnish blank certificates to local officials. If these are numbered the supervising agency may require each particular certificate used to be accounted for. This is a useful arrangement for avoiding abuses. Very frequently the state agency requires reports of the certificates issued. Sometimes this consists of a mere list of names. By far the best practice, however, is to require duplicate certificates to be sent in together with an account of the evidence submitted. Some supervising agencies have the power to prescribe the exact sorts of evidence which will be accepted. The best arrangement requires the local issuing officer to send an exact report of the evidence submitted in each particular case. If the state agency feels that this is insufficient it may have the power of revoking the certificate. Such a system offers good assurance that the same standards will be enforced throughout the whole state. A few state supervising agencies have the power to appoint issuing officers and to remove them in case of inefficiency. This makes for better enforcement. In any case there should be a number of traveling supervisors connected with the state agency who make frequent visits to the local officers to inspect their work and to answer questions when difficulties arise.

In issuing certificates five requirements are more or less generally enforced. The first of these is the application of the child in person accompanied by one parent or guardian. Although it occasionally happens that permits are granted by mail this represents a very bad practice. When the child and his parent appear in person before the issuing officer it is possible to discuss the situation with them and possibly to advise the child to return to school. Where the law gives the issuing officer a certain amount of discretion in issuing certificates such an interview may help to answer questions of economic need.

A second very usual requirement is a promise of employment which often must be given on forms furnished by the office which issues certificates. There are several reasons for requiring such a promise. In states where children are required to attend school unless they are at work it prevents a child from obtaining a certificate merely as an excuse to leave school. Again where physical examinations are given a promise of employment helps the examining physician to judge whether the child is physically able to hold the particular job for which he is applying. Finally the issuing officer is often thus able to prevent children from entering forbidden occupations.

Experience has shown that the most difficult requirement to enforce concerns the child's age. The best evidenec of age is a birth certificate. This, however, is often difficult to obtain. The registration of births in this country has been very incomplete in the past although at present it is rapidly improving. The experience of government inspectors during the enforcement of the First Federal Child-Labor Act showed that birth certificates were secured in only two-tenths of one per cent of the children applying for certificates in North Carolina and in three-tenths of one per cent in South Carolina (15). It is the best practice to insist upon a birth certificate and only when the impossibility of producing it has been clearly proved to accept less valid evidence. This was the practice which the federal authorities adopted when enforcing the First National Child-Labor Act (15). Next to the birth certificate in value is the baptisimal certificate. After this come other documents such as Bible records, contemporary letters, passports, or school records. These are very much inferior to birth and baptisimal certificates since they are easily forged. Only when all better records fail may a certificate of physical age be acceptable. Such a certificate should be issued by a school or public health physician and should indicate the exact evidence such as height and weight upon which the physician bases his judgment.

Certain standards of physical health represent a fourth common requirement. There is much diversity among state laws on this point. Some states do not require a physical examination at all, some require it only for certain occupations or leave it to the discretion of the issuing officer while some require it in all cases. The last certainly represents the best practice. Only designated physicians should be authorized to make these examinations. By concentrating the work in the hands of a few specialists much higher efficiency is attained. In no case should the examining be done by the child's private physician. The standards of this work can be improved if the state supervising agency issues a blank with

detailed instructions about the tests to be made.
Experience has shown that where this is done the
physician is less likely to give a certificate after
a very cursory examination. Defects should be
corrected before a permanent employment certificate is issued.

The attainment of a certain educational standard is a fifth requirement, which appears in
many state laws. This may take two forms.
Either the child may be required to complete a
certain school grade or occasionally he may be
subjected to an examination by the issuing officer. The former probably represents the better
practice although grade standards undoubtedly
differ somewhat between cities and even between
different school in the same city. Some provision
should be made for the issuing of school records
during the summer when the schools themselves
are closed. One good practice is to keep a file in
the office of the superintendent of schools containing the records of all the children of all the
schools in the city. Where the law allows mentally defective children to be excused from
school before they have completed the educational requirements the existence of mental defects should be determined by psychological
examinations and not by the mere judgment of
a teacher or principal.

An employment certificate should be valid only for a particular job and the employer should be required by law to return the certificate to the issuing office if the child leaves his employment. This seems to be the only possible way of enforcing school attendance among unemployed children of the legal working age since otherwise the child might obtain his certificate, hold a position for a few days, and then leave it. The school-attendance department would then have no way of knowing that this child was neither in school nor at work. Another reason for requiring a new certificate for every job is the possibility thus afforded of requiring another physical examination. If the child is thus examined before each new job a constant check may be kept on his condition. It would be better still if all employed children could be re-examined periodically even when no change of job was in question. Besides regular certificates temporary ones are sometimes issued when there is a delay in getting evidence of age or while physical defects are being corrected. Vacation permits should be issued on a special form.

The subject of school-attendance enforcement is closely related to the question of child labor. Indeed they are frequently united into one department. The appointment of attendance officers is often required by state laws and sometimes the state department of education has some supervision over the work of local attendance authorities. It may, for instance, prescribe the forms to be used and require periodic reports.

The school census is the only reasonably efficient method of locating children not in school. Such a census may be made by teachers, attendance officers, the police, or by special enumerators. It is best made under the supervision of the school-attendance department. Usually it is taken every year, although a better practice is to have a permanent census. This differs from the other in that enumerators are at work constantly bringing the census up to date. The best practice calls for a special card for every child or at least for every family. When the census has been taken it is checked against the school records and against the names on employment certificates. Names on the census report which do not appear on either of the other records represent children who are either not attending school or who are employed without a work permit.

In order to have child-labor laws administered efficiently it is necessary to develop a good system of factory inspection. Usually this is regarded as a state function and the inspectors work directly under some state agency, generally as a part of the state labor department. The inspectors have authority to visit all factories in the state and employers are generally required by state law to keep all employment certificates on file for reference. The inspector when he visits a factory may interview all children who appear to be of certificate age and obtain from them their names and other identifying data. He then checks these facts against the certificates which the employer has on file. If variations are discovered the employer may be required to discharge the child immediately and in more serious cases he may be prosecuted. The investigator can visit the factory at night to make sure that children are not being employed at illegal hours.

The administration of child-labor laws is aided by good industrial inspection in two ways. The inspectors can educate the employers in the requirements of state legislation and in case the latter prove refractory they can prosecute the case in court. The modern practice is to lay more emphasis on educational than on legal measures. For although prosecution can sometimes secure an external obedience to the letter of the law, only good educational work can secure the genuine coöperation of the employer.

Street work for children is a separate problem which was not made a subject for legal regulation until long after other sorts of child labor had been restricted by law. Although city ordinances had been passed previously, the first state law regarding street work was the New York law of 1903.

The federal census of 1920 sets the number of newspaper sellers between ten and sixteen at 20,513. This probably understates the real number very considerably. The Children's Bureau on the basis of a survey of several cities states that the census data "would more nearly approximate the actual figure if multiplied by 2" (9). Even then they would not include children under ten who make up ten or twenty per cent of all newspaper boys. Add to these the number of children engaged as peddlers, bootblacks, and in other street occupations and it will be seen that the number of children engaged in street work is very considerable.

A very common street trade is selling newspapers. While the age at which children enter nearly all other occupations is constantly increasing, this is not true of the newsboys. In eight surveys (9) assembled by the Children's Bureau boys of six and seven were found selling papers in every city studied. From one-fifth to one-tenth of the boys were under ten. In two cities more than one-half of the newsboys had not reached their twelfth birthday.

The above studies reveal that the boys worked on an average of about 16 hours a week. This was probably long enough to interfere considerably with school work. The effect on the health of the children is presumably rather detrimental. Instead of enjoying an afternoon of healthy play followed by a warm dinner and bed at an early hour, many of the boys were forced to spend long hours on the streets in all sorts of weather, often contended themselves with a sandwich or "hot dog" for supper, while frequently they were deprived of needed sleep.

The most convincing argument against newspaper selling for young boys, however, it its moral effect. Conditions in the distribution rooms where children receive their papers to sell were often found to be highly immoral. The effect of this upon the boy is shown by the very high proportion who had been brought before juvenile courts.

Many have felt that economic reasons make street work necessary for newsboys. These studies, however, fail to bear out this assumption. The weekly earnings of the boys were small, the median amount varying between one and five dollars in different cities. Although an economic urge was present in a great many cases, actual economic necessity was not the chief reason for selling papers given by the majority of the boys included in the Children's Bureau studies.

Newspaper carriers delivering papers along fixed routes compare very favorably with the street peddlers. They were found to be a little older than the newsboys, they included a smaller proportion of delinquents, and they came generally from better families. Delivering papers does not seem to involve any particular moral hazard nor to interfere notably with school work or health.

Quite a few boys among street traders are peddlers. Some of them act as helpers to hucksters while others go from door to door selling small articles or stand about in public buildings or on street corners plying their trade. A large proportion of these boys worked every day and had been at their trade for at least a year. The majority worked two hours a day or more on school days.

Contrary to impression the number of bootblacks does not appear to be diminishing very rapidly. According to the Children's Bureau study the average age of these child workers is 12. Although the number of bootblacks is much less than the number of newsboys the two trades are open to very similar objections. They both probably interfere with school work and have a deleterious effect on health.

Only 11 states have state-wide laws affecting children engaged in street work. Although municipal ordinances exist in many cities the problem is in general not being efficiently met. The laws are not adequate. Besides this, regulations concerning street trades are probably less well enforced than other child-labor laws. It is, however, perfectly possible to enforce them if a proper effort is made. Permits should be required and these should be issued by some person who is in sympathy with modern child-welfare ideals. Often they are issued by the officer who is in charge of other employment certificates. This is perhaps the ideal arrangement. More emphasis must be laid on frequent inspection than in the case of the enforcement of regulations applying to factories. Although good results occasionally follow when the police are in charge of regulations applying to street trades, probably the best arrangement is to put the work in the hands of the agency which issues the certificates. It is often been found useful to require street workers to wear a badge as a sign that they have been granted certificates. This requirement is not very effective unless precautions are taken to prevent workers exchanging badges.

It may be seen from this brief review that the problem of child labor is by no means fully solved in the United States. Although many of the glaring abuses of a generation or two ago have been abolished, much more remains to be done. The problem will not be fully solved until every child in this country has been assured the opportunity to enjoy the free and happy childhood which is his right.

## BIBLIOGRAPHY

(1) Brown, Sara A. and others: *Children working in the sugar beet fields of certain districts of the South Platte Valley, Colorado.* New York, National Child Labor Committee, 1925. 167 p.
A study under the auspices of the National Child Labor Committee. Children were found to be working long hours and school attendance was poorly enforced.

(2) Burdge, Howard Griffith: *Our boys; a study of the 245,000 sixteen, seventeen, and eighteen year old employed boys of the state of New York.* Albany, J. B. Lyon Company, 1921. viii, 345 p.
Six-sevenths of boys of this age were out of school.

Less than 15 per cent were forced to leave school
on account of poverty.

(3) Byrne, Harriet A.: *Child labor in representative
tobacco-growing areas.* Washington, D. C., U. S.
Gov't Printing Office, 1926.  v, 42 p.  (Chil-
dren's Bureau Publication No. 155.)
A study of selected areas in Kentucky, South
Carolina, Virginia, and the Connecticut Valley.

(4) Channing, Alice: *Child labor in fruit and hop growing districts of the northern Pacific Coast.* Washington, D. C., U. S. Gov't Printing Office, 1926.
v, 52 p. (Children's Bureau Publication No. 151.)
Surveys conditions in Washington and Oregon.

(5) Channing, Alice: *Child labor on Maryland truck
farms.* Washington D. C., U. S. Gov't Printing
Office, 1923.  v. 52 p.  (Children's Bureau Publication No. 123.)
A study of four Maryland counties.

(6) Fuller, Raymond G.: *Child labor and the constitu-
tion.*  New York, Thomas Y. Crowell Company,
1923.  xvi, 323 p.
Possibly the best comprehensive treatment of the
whole subject.

(7) Fuller, Raymond G. and Strong, Mabel A.: *Child
labor in Massachusetts; an inquiry under the auspices of the Massachusetts Child Labor Committee.* Boston, Massachusetts Child Labor Committee, 1926.  170 p.
An excellent treatment of the question in one
state.

(8) Gray, Edith S.: *Industrial accidents to employed
minors in Wisconsin, Massachusetts, and New
Jersey.* Washington, D. C., U. S. Gov't Printing Office, 1926.  v, 119 p.  (Children's Bureau
Publication No. 152.)

"Within 12 months 7478 industrial injuries oc-
curred to employed minors under 21 years of age
in these three states, 38 resulting fatally and 920
in partial disability for life."

(9) McGill, Nettie P.: *Children in street work*. Washington, D. C., U. S. Gov't Printing Office, 1928.
ix, 353 p.  (Children's Bureau Publication No.
183.)
Studies of eight cities.

(10) Merritt, Ella Arvilla:  *Legal regulation of the employment of minors 16 years of age and over*.
Washington, D. C., U. S. Gov't Printing Office,
n. d.  26 p.
Gives laws in effect July 1, 1924.

(11) National Child Labor Committee: *Rural child wel-
fare; an inquiry by the National Child Labor
Committee based upon conditions in West Virginia*.
New York, The Macmillan Company, 1922.
355 p.
A collection of reports by half a dozen experts.

(12) Paradise, Viola I.:  *Child labor and the work of
mothers in oyster and shrimp canning communities
on the Gulf Coast*.  Washington, D. C., U. S.
Gov't Printing Office, 1922.  114 p.  (Children's
Bureau Publication No. 98.)
On account of the irregular character of this industry it has proved very difficult to regulatte.

(13) Skinner, Mary:  *Child labor in New Jersey.  Part
2.  Children engaged in industrial home work*.
Washington, D. C., U. S. Gov't Printing Office,
1928.  v, 62 p.  (Children's Bureau Publication
No. 185.)
A study of industrial home work in 12 selected
communities.

(14) Thompson, Laura A.: *References on child labor and minors in industry, 1916-1924*. Washington, D. C., U. S. Gov't Printing Office, 1925. vi, 153 p. (Children's Bureau Publication No. 147.)
An excellent bibliography.

(15) U. S. Children's Bureau: *Administration of the First Federal Child-Labor Law*. Washington, D. C., U. S. Gov't Printing Office, 1921. 197 p. (Children's Bureau Publication No. 78.)
Throws much light on conditions of child workers in various states.

(16) U. S. Children's Bureau: *Child labor and the work of mothers on Norfolk truck farms*. Washington, D. C., U. S. Gov't Printing Office, 1924. iv, 27 p. (Children's Bureau Publication No. 130.)
Nearly all the children were negroes.

(17) U. S. Children's Bureau: *Child labor in North Dakota*. Washington, D. C., U. S. Gov't Printing Office, 1923. v, 67 p. (Children's Bureau Publication No. 129.)
A study of six counties and three cities.

(18) U. S. Children's Bureau: *Child labor in the United States; ten questions answered*. Fourth Edition. Washington, D. C., U. S. Gov't Printing Office, 1926. 36 p. (Children's Bureau Publication No. 114.)
A brief compilation of information on child labor.

(19) U. S. Children's Bureau: *Child labor; outlines for study. Fifth edition*. Washington, D. C., U. S. Gov't Printing Office, 1926. vi, 61 p. (Children's Bureau Publication, No. 93.)
A very convenient summary.

(20) U. S. Children's Bureau: *Industrial home work of children; a study made in Providence, Pawtucket,*

*and Central Falls, R. I.* Washington, D. C.
U. S. Gov't Printing Office, 1924. 80 p. (Children's Bureau Publication No. 100.)
On account of the obvious difficulty of supervision this sort of work is subject to many abuses.

(21) U. S. Children's Bureau: *Physical standards for working children. Preliminary report of the committee appointed by the Children's Bureau of the U. S. Department of Labor to formulate standards of normal development and sound health for the use of physicians in examining children entering employment and children at work.* Washington, D. C., U. S. Gov't Printing Office, 1926. 24 p. (Children's Bureau Publication No. 79, revised.)
Includes synopsis of legislation in force August 15, 1926.

(22) U. S. Children's Bureau: *Report of the Chief, Children's Bureau to the Secretary of Labor; fiscal year ended June* 30, 1923. Washington, D. C., U. S. Gov't Printing Office, 1923. iii, 38 p.
Contains results of factory inspection in Georgia by federal officials.

(23) U. S. Children's Bureau: *The welfare of children in cotton-growing areas of Texas.* Washington, D. C., U. S. Gov't Printing Office, 1924. v, 83 p. (Children's Bureau Publication No. 134.)
A study in Hill and Rusk Counties.

(24) U. S. Children's Bureau: *Work of children on truck and small-fruit farms in southern New Jersey.* Washington, D. C., U. S. Gov't Printing Office, 1924. v, 58 p. (Children's Bureau Publication No. 132.)
The children were mostly Italian, partly resident and partly migratory workers.

(25) Williams, Dorothy and Skinner, Mary E.: *Work of children on Illinois farms.* Washington, D. C., U. S. Gov't Printing Office, 1926.  v, 48 p. (Children's Bureau Publication No. 168.)
A study of four counties.

(26) Woodbury, Helen Sumner: *Administration of Child-labor laws. Part 5. Standards applicable to the administration of employment certificate systems.* Washington, D. C., U. S. Gov't Printing Office, 1924.  vii, 227 p.  (Children's Bureau Publication No. 133.)
An excellent reference.  Contains tabular summary of laws.

(27) Woodbury, Helen Sumner: *The working children of Boston, a study of child labor under a modern system of legal regulation.* Washington, D. C., U. S. Gov't Printing Office, 1922.  viii, 374 p. (Children's Bureau Publication No. 89.)
A very thorough study.  Includes case histories.

# CHAPTER XI

## *The Dependent Child*

The history of organized work on behalf of the dependent child in this country goes back almost two centuries. In 1729 the Ursuline Sisters opened a home for children left orphans as a result of the Indian massacres. From this time on homes were opened with increasing frequency. The period following the wave of immigration around 1850 and the period following the Civil War saw an especially rapid growth of the movement. Although, as will be seen, the institution is now being gradually replaced by other methods of child care, it is still society's most common answer to the problem of the dependent child. In 1923 the United States Census Bureau knew of over one hundred forty thousand children in child-caring homes—a figure which represents 64.2 per cent of the entire known number of dependent children.

In the meantime, however, the placing of these children in boarding or free homes has been growing by leaps and bounds. This movement was foreshadowed to some extent by the indenture system of the English common law. The New York Children's Aid Society, organized in 1853 by Charles Loring Brace was the first attempt to organize child placement on a large scale as an answer to the problem of the dependent child. The succeeding decades saw the development of similar societies all over the country. These early organizations were characterized by rather loose standards according to modern ideals. Investigation before placement and continuing supervision were not well organized. But as time went on methods became greatly standardized and improved. Eighteen per cent of the dependent children in our country enumerated in the census of 1923 were receiving foster-home care.

For many years the relative advantages of the institution and the family home were heatedly discussed. It was not until the close of the century that the relative functions of these two methods began to be recognized and a committee report presented at the 1899 meeting of the National Conference of Charities and Corrections by the Honorable Thomas M. Mulry is important as representing the crystallized opinion of half a century on this problem.

Modern work for the dependent child may be said to date from the White House Conference on Dependent Children called by President Roosevelt in January, 1909, shortly before he left office. This meeting, which brought together the most representative opinion of the entire country, adopted a series of resolutions which have now become the classic statement of the principles governing the care of the dependent child. The most important of these principles is expressed in the often quoted statement: "Home life is the highest and finest product of civilization. It is the great motive force of mind and character. Children should not be deprived of it except for urgent and compelling reasons." These same principles were reaffirmed in 1919 by the Washington and Regional Conferences on Child Welfare called by the Children's Bureau.

Modern work with the dependent child is merely an attempt to put these ideals into practice. It is recognized that except under extraordinary conditions the ideal place for the child is its own home. Therefore every attempt is made to avoid the removal of the child. It is recognized further that poverty alone is not a valid reason for separating the child from its mother. This fact has brought about the passage of the so-called *mothers' pension laws* which are now almost universal in this country. Secondly, when the child must be removed from its parental home an attempt is usually made to place him with some private family because this is the closest approximation to the family life which the White House Conference had considered to be the ideal thing for the child. This principle has inspired the modern movement for child placement. Finally, when placement in a family is impossible, and the child must be entered in an institution an effort is made through some form of the "group system" to approximate within the institution the spirit of family life. Thus the principle that family life is essential for the proper upbringing of the child is applied through the three great developments characteristic of the modern treatment of the dependent child; namely, the movement for family rehabilitation, the boarding home idea, and the cottage-type of institution.

Few new ideas in the field of social legislation have won public approval with the rapidity with which the principles of public aid for mothers with dependent children, the so-called mothers' pension laws, have been adopted. This legislation was foreshadowed as early as 1906 when the juvenile courts in some counties of

California granted aid to children in their own homes. An Oklahoma law of 1908 provided for school scholarships to be given by the counties to the children of widowed mothers. But the real origin of mothers' pension laws must be placed in 1911 when the legislatures of Missouri and Illinois passed laws of this sort. By 1913, 21 states had enacted such laws. At the present writing 44 states, Alaska, Hawaii, and the District of Columbia have mother's pension legislation.

Wide variation is shown in the details of these laws. In a few states only widows are eligible to receive such aid. In half a dozen states the language is general and any mother with dependent children is eligible. The other states provide in detail what mothers may receive the benefits of the law. There is wide variation of practice in regard to mothers whose husbands are divorced, incapacitated, or confined in prison or institutions for the insane, feeble-minded, or epileptic. The term *mother* in some states includes relatives or guardians on whom the child is dependent and sometimes expectant mothers.

State laws generally contain provisions to prevent the abuse of mothers' pension acts. There is generally a residence requirement so that the floating population of the country will not receive the benefits of this law. Some states limit the granting of aid to women who do not own real property or who own not more than a specified amount. Some states make the granting of aid conditional upon the mother's ability to care properly for the children, the proper education of the children, or other similar conditions.

The prevailing tendency is to allow aid to be granted until the child is 16 years of age. Michigan and Tennessee set the age at 17 while a few states set it at 14 or 15.

In some states there is a specified maximum of aid to be granted, this depending upon the size of the family. The best legislation is represented by the laws of some half dozen states which leave the amount to be granted to the discretion of the supervising agency.

Mother's aid laws are generally administered by a local agency. In about one-half the states this is the juvenile court. In the balance it is generally some board concerned with child welfare or the administration of relief although in some cases a special agency has been established. In about 10 states these local agencies work in coöperation with state administrative bureaus and in more than half the states there is some sort of state supervision of the work.

Although it will be seen from the above that mother's pension legislation is now almost uni-

versal in this country, there are very wide variations in the extent to which these laws are put
into practice. Some of the states are barely
scratching the surface of the problem while even
the most progressive states have probably not
met it really adequately. It follows that the need
is not so much for better legislation as for the
wider application of existing laws and the increased appropriations which should make this
possible.

Not only is the number of children receiving
aid less than it should be but the amount of aid
granted is probably often much less than the
best case-work standards would dictate. The only
way of meeting the need adequately is to set the
standard of welfare which the home should receive and then to determine by careful budgetary
studies the amount of aid necessary to bring the
family up to this standard. While it would evidently be unwise to countenance useless luxury
in homes receiving aid, the standard aimed at
should not be below that of the working class
of the community. The spirit of the best case
work is expressed by the statement of an administrative official who spoke with pride of the
fact that children of families receiving aid in
his jurisdiction were undistinguishable by their

dress from the other children of the school which they attended.

Even with the best mother's pension legislation there will always be a certain number of children who must be removed from their parental home. This includes orphans and children whose homes are unsuitable either on account of the extremely low mentality of the parents or their immorality. For such children modern social work strives to provide a family home, for it is felt that the nearest approximation to home life is furnished by this method.

Broadly speaking there are three types of family homes in which dependent children may be placed. The *free home*, as the name implies, is one in which the child is placed without the payment of board. Such a home may be found among persons who are willing to accept the child as a pure act of kindness. Again, the child may be placed with relatives. The adoptive home is a free home in which the arrangement is made permanent by legal means. The second general category of family home is the *boarding home* where the child is kept in return for the payment of money. Finally in the *wage home* the child pays his own board by working for his foster parents.

Child placement is regarded as a highly specialized branch of social work and is generally entrusted to a separate agency or at least to a separate bureau or department. As has been stated above, the pioneer work in child placing was done by private societies. In recent years there has been a tendency to organize this work under public-welfare agencies. Probably both public and private bodies will always continue to work side by side in the field but the importance of the public agency is at present constantly increasing.

Whatever body undertakes placement work certain principles apply. A point of great importance is the selection and training of a competent personnel. There is a growing tendency to insist upon professional training in a school of social work for all, while executive positions are generally restricted to persons with college degrees. The location and layout of the central office is also important. It should be in a readily accessible place and should contain a sufficient number of private offices to be used in the highly delicate interviews involved in placement work.

The problem of financing placement work is easily solved by public agencies since they are supplied from public funds. A Children's Bureau survey (11) showed that among the private agencies the most common sources of revenue were donations, contributions, subsidies from public funds, community chests, and reimbursements from the parents and relatives of children placed out. Among the expenditures the largest item of expense was board for children which accounted for two-fifths of the total. Salaries came next, forming about one-third of the total expenditures, while clothing, travel, health, and miscellaneous expenses accounted for the balance.

Before the agency can begin actual placement work it is necessary for it to be in contact with a number of possible foster homes where children may be placed. Modern practice is emphasizing this department of the work more and more and the best plan is to employ special workers as "home finders" whose duty is to discover suitable homes. There are many ways of doing this. Carefully worded newspaper advertisements usually bring a large response but the experience of many agencies has been that among these only a very small proportion prove satisfactory. A certain number may be located by radio appeals and by speeches before women's clubs. Suggestions by foster parents in other boarding homes is another very fruitful source.

Finally the agency may always count on a number of unsought applications.

A placement agency of high standards will be forced to reject a large proportion of applications among the suggested foster homes. To be satisfactory such a home must offer certain definite things. The physical conditions must be satisfactory. Certain obvious standards of cleanliness and comfort must be attained. The family income must be sufficient to assure a continuance of these conditions. A less obvious but far more important requirement concerns the personalities of the foster parents. They must be intelligent and coöperative and able to deal with children sympathetically. Finally, they must be able to care for the religious life of the child. Catholic children should always be placed with Catholic foster parents and Protestant children with Protestant foster parents. Modern practice emphasizes these intangible things far more than the mere physical conditions of the prospective home.

The children handled by a placement agency may be referred to it either through legal procedure or through a voluntary arrangement. Under the former plan the agency may be appointed as legal guardian of the child or the child may be committed to it through parental

surrender or court action. Under the latter plan
a parent or other guardian gives the child into
the custody of the agency informally while re-
taining strict legal control. Where the child is
committed to the agency by public authority
there is generally some provision for its maintenance out of the public funds or by help
through court order. Where the child is given
to the care of the agency by its parent or guardian there should be a clear understanding about
its maintenance and the understanding should
be committed to writing. The policy of most
agencies is to insist upon payment of the child's
board by the parent or guardian wherever this
can be done without causing hardship to the
latter.

An important function of a child-placing
agency is the preservation of home life where it
is possible. The day is passed when a child is
considered suitable for placement merely because his parent says so. The larger part of the
applications coming before some agencies are
refused on the grounds that it would not be for
the best interests of the child to be moved from
his home.

The investigation of applications for placement is a function which is often given to
workers who specialize in this type of work

alone. When an application has been made to an office the investigator visits the home and the final decision is not reached until after a most careful study and discussion of the case at a special conference.

Preferably the child should be given a complete physical and psychological examination and remediable physical defects should be carefully corrected. The psychological examination will determine whether or not the child will be capable of profiting by school training and will guide the agency in making the placement.

Having gathered this information the agency is in a position to make the placement intelligently. There should be an explicit understanding concerning the child's attendance at church and school, the amount of work he will be expected to do, and any necessary arrangement about spending money or wages. The religious welfare of the child should receive careful consideration and generally speaking children should always be placed with foster parents of the same religious denomination.

The duty of the agency making the placement does not end when the child has been put in a foster home. There is need of careful and regular supervision. The worker from the agency must visit the foster home frequently and there inquire both from the child and the foster parents how well the arrangement is succeeding. Where there is friction between the child and the other members of the family the worker can tactfully discuss the causes of it and when possible remove them. In the occasional case where this is not possible the child must be removed and another placement made.

Sometimes a placement, particularly in a free family home will turn out so successfully that the parents will desire to adopt the child. Adoption is a process by which the natural parents of a child relinquish their legal title to it in favor of the adopting parents. Adoption legislation has undergone important changes in the United States during the past few years. The older tendency was to look upon this as purely a legal matter so that little effort was made to find whether adoption was advisable in the particular case and the rôle of the court was limited to declaring that the proper legal formalities had been met.

The newer attitudes focuses attention more upon the personalities of the child and his foster parents than upon the purely technical and legal side. It is beginning to be considered the best practice to give jurisdiction over adoption cases to some socialized court such as a juvenile or a domestic relations court. For only courts of this type are likely to have both the socialized viewpoint and the special technical assistance necessary to make a social and scientific study of the child and of the home into which he is to be adopted.

Whether or not the court in question be of the socialized type, the adoption procedure follows largely certain standardized methods—a petition filed by the adopting parents, notice to the child's parents, their consent and the judicial degree.

The most important recent tendency is the state supervision of all adoptions. For example, in Minnesota, North Dakota, Oregon, and Virginia provision is made that the state must investigate before a degree is granted. Still more significant is the Minnesota law which provides that the state Board of Control must be notified concerning all child placements by the child caring organizations. Somewhat similar legislation exists in North Dakota.

The child who is deprived of a normal home suffers an irreparable loss. But modern placement work, if carried out carefully and efficiently, can supply this loss in some degree. It cannot perhaps restore the child's own home.

But it can place him in healthful and wholesome surroundings where he will have an opportunity of developing into a good and useful citizen.

## BIBLIOGRAPHY

(1) Hall, W. Clark and Hall, Justin Clarke: *The law of adoption and guardianship of infants; with special reference to courts of summary jurisdiction, together with the Legitimacy Act, 1926.* London, Butterworth & Company, 1928. 171 p.
Contains the texts of the English Adoption, Guardianship, and Legitimacy Acts.

(2) Lundberg, Emma O.: *Public aid to mothers with dependent children; extent and 'fundamental principles.* Washington, D. C., U. S. Gov't Printing Office, 1928, iii, 24 p. (Children's Bureau Publication No. 162 Revised.)
A brief treatment of mother's pension legislation.

(3) Nesbitt, Florence: *Standards of public aid to children in their own homes.* Washington, D. C., U. S. Gov't Printing Office, 1923. vii, 145 p. (Children's Bureau Publication No. 118.)
A study of current practice.

(4) O'Grady, John: "A preliminary survey of Catholic child-caring work in the United States." *Cath. Char. Rev.,* 7:141-43, April, 1923. An interesting account of Catholic work.

(5) Peck, Emelyn Foster: *Adoption laws in the United States; a summary of the development of adoption legislation and significant features of adoption statutes, with the text of selected laws.* Washington, D. C., U. S. Gov't Printing Office, 1925.

v, 51 p.   (Children's Bureau Publication No. 148.)

A review of the legislation.

(6) Theis, Sophie van Senden: *How foster children turn out; a study and critical analysis of 901 children who were placed in foster homes by the State Charities Aid Association.* New York, State Charities Aid Association, 1924. 239 p. (State Charities Aid Association of New York. Publication No. 165.)

Only 12 per cent of the children were still "definitely at odds with society or still needed protection or training such as is given by a State institution or other official body."

(7) Thurston, Henry W.: "How much child dependency is there in the United States?" *Proceedings Nat. Conf. of Social Work, 53rd Annual Session,* 1926, pp. 148-51.

This writer estimates the total at six hundred thousand.

(8) U. S. Children's Bureau: *Foster-home care for dependent children.* Washington, D. C., U. S. Gov't Printing Office, 1924. v, 275 p. (Children's Bureau Publication No. 136.)

A brief summary of modern principles.

(9) U. S. Children's Bureau: *Handbook for the use of boards of directors, superintendents, and staffs of institutions for dependent children.* Washington, D. C., U. S. Gov't Printing Office, 1927. vi, 129 p. (Children's Bureau Publication No. 170.)

Full of valuable suggestions. Chapters on "Admissions," "Discharge," and "Aftercare" contain principles applicable to placement work.

(10) U. S. Children's Bureau: *Laws relating to "mothers' pensions" in the United States, Canada, Denmark,*

*and New Zealand.* Washington, D. C., U. S.
Gov't Printing Office, 1919. 316 p.   (Children's
Bureau Publication No. 63.)
A review of the legislation.

(11) U. S. Children's Bureau: *The work of child-placing
agencies. Part I. A social study of ten agencies
caring for dependent children.* by Katharine P.
Hewins and L. Josephine Webster; *Part II.
Health supervision of children placed in foster
homes,* by Mary L. Evans. Washington, D. C.,
U. S. Gov't Printing Office, 1927.  ix, 223 p.
(Children's Bureau Publication No. 171.)
A study of current practice.

# CHAPTER XII

## *Child-Caring Institutions*

The importance of the institution as a means of caring for children is declining constantly. Yet few would be willing to predict a day in which it would entirely disappear. The normal home is undoubtedly the best place for the normal child but many children are not normal. Some of these need highly specialized types of care, implying specially trained personnel or special equipment. For such children the institution remains a necessity. Modern practice, therefore, prescribes the boarding home for most dependent children. But for the delinquent, the deaf, blind, crippled, and low-grade feeble-minded as well as the children with grave behavior difficulties or physical defects the institution is, often at least, the only feasible treatment.

The recognition of home life as the ideal training for children has, moreover, influenced the institution itself. There has been a very conscious effort to bring the spirit of the normal home into it. This tendency finds its fullest expression in what is known as the *cottage type* of child caring home. Under this form of organization the children are divided into small groups each living in a separate cottage and an effort is made to approximate family life in each group. One person is in charge of each cottage continually and thus is able to know intimately the children under her charge. Naturally the smaller the group, the more closely home life can be imitated. The system works best where the group consists of not more than 15 or 20 children, although actually very much larger groups occur.

In the pure cottage system each unit is entirely independent of the others except that they are all under a single central administration. Not only does the group live in its own building with its own recreation hall and study room but it has its own kitchen and dining room as well. This is particularly advantageous when the group includes older girls since it affords an opportunity for practical instruction in home economics. However, many people feel that in ordinary cases the economy of a central kitchen and dining room for the whole institution more than compensate for the possible loss in group spirit.

In spite of the obvious advantages of the cottage type of institution many of our child-caring homes are still of the old-fashioned congregate type in which the entire population of the institution live in common and there is no attempt at classification beyond a division on the basis of sex. Even some new institutions are being built on the congregate plan. One advantage claimed is that of economy. The congregate institution is cheaper to build and since it requires a smaller staff, cheaper to maintain.

The group system is a sort of compromise between the other two. It divides the population of the institution into small groups separated as much as possible from each other, but not possessing separate buildings. The group plan often represents an attempt to get the benefits of the cottage system in an institution which was built with the congregate plan in view.  (6)

To whichever type a given institution belongs it is very necessary that it should keep abreast of the constantly improving methods of institutional care. In the case of publicly supported homes this is generally brought about by some type of state supervision. This varies from mere power of inspection and recommendation on the part of some state board to complete administrative control by a highly organized state welfare department. The practice seems to incline strongly in the direction of the latter type. Private institutions are naturally less subject to state control. There is a tendency, however, to compel even these institutions to reach certain standards. In some states this is brought about by the refusal of state aid to those who fall below the standards while in others a license is required before any child-caring institution can be opened.

In many institutions, even those under rather centralized public control, it is a great advantage to have an interested and efficient board of trustees in charge. In the case of a private institution such a board may be self-perpetuating or it may be appointed or elected by the body which sponsors the institution. The members should be carefully chosen to represent the different localities and racial or religious groups from which the institution derives support. They should also represent various types of specialized training and ability so that if complications of a technical nature arise, the institution can have the benefit of trained advice.

An efficient staff is essential. An old-fashioned congregate institution in the hands of a progressive and well trained staff will probably be better than the most modern cottage-type home whose staff does not appreciate the ideals of present day child-caring work. There has been a subtle but very real change in the character of institutional staffs in the course of the last 25 or 30 years. It is now recognized that the care of the child requires technical skill of a high order. The present practice is to require a good educational background and specialized training as well as experience in the executive head of the institution while the balance of the staff must be carefully chosen and must be intelligent and coöperative. Too much pains cannot be taken to secure an efficient superintendent. While the governing body determines general policies it must depend upon him for the technical information upon which these policies are based as well as for efficiency in carrying them out.

Whether the institutions in question be of the congregate, group, or cottage type certain general principles must be observed in the layout and construction of the plant. It is quite evident that the ideal location is not to be found in the midst of a great city. Not only will the children miss the quiet and fresh air of the country but the price of land will often prevent the institution from acquiring sufficient grounds for its purposes. On the other hand, when it is located too far out in the country it may be too much isolated from the life of the community. The ideal location seems to be somewhere in the suburbs close enough to the city to enjoy the conveniences of urban life and yet far enough away from thickly settled districts to secure sufficient room for the children to play.

Many institutions find it advantageous to have a small farm where the boys may be taught farming as a prevocational subject. If sufficient land is available the institution may save money by raising its own fruit and vegetables. In such a case, however, there should be sufficient hired help. The staff must not yield to the temptation of turning the boys into farm laborers, thus depriving them of necessary training on other lines.

The plan of the buildings will naturally depend on the type of the institution itself. The essential point is that the buildings should be healthful and that they should not hamper the work of the staff in training the child. The former requirement calls for fireproof construction unless small one-story cottages are used in which case the fire hazards may never be serious. It requires, further, that the rooms be light and airy with a window area equal to at least one-fifth of the floor area and that the sleeping rooms allow at least 500 cubic feet of air space per child. The water supply should be from a source known to be safe. If the institution is not connected with a city sewage system its own system should be planned after consultation with a specialist on this subject.

The effect of the institution on the personality of the child is even more important than its effect on his health. This fact must be taken into consideration in planning the buildings. Sleeping rooms which are used by six or eight children are much preferable to large dormitories. A better arrangement still in the case of older children is to provide each with a separate room.

There should be, again, plenty of room for recreation. The indoor playroom should preferably not be in the basement. Finally, comfortable accommodations for the staff will aid in securing a better personnel and will impose less nervous strain upon it.

The day is far gone when an institution accepted a child merely on the basis of an application endorsed by some respectable person. The last chapter has explained the necessity of case investigation before any child is removed from his own home. Modern standards require that such a study shall be made in every case before a child is admitted to an institution. It may be made either by some social agency or by a worker attached to the institution itself. In any case a detailed social history should be kept on file. This will aid in understanding the child himself and in determining the question of discharge.

Each child on being admitted should be given a complete physical examination. This also should be made a part of his official record and remediable defects should be corrected at once. Many institutions require a quarantine period of a couple of weeks following admission to prevent the spread of communicable disease. Other institutions feel that a shorter period is satisfactory provided a careful social history shows no contacts with such disease prior to admission. In many modern institutions, however, the children mingle freely with those outside and in such a case the quarantine becomes purposeless. In any case care must be taken that the isolation period is not too depressing for the child.

The best modern institutions feel that psychological tests are not less necessary than physical examination. Such tests provide a basis for understanding the child and for advising in regard to vocational training. In general the better the institution understands the individual child and the more it attempts to make its training fit the particular case the better does it accomplish its purpose.

The real function of the institution is not to provide safe care for the children over a difficult period. It is not a "refuge"; it is not an "asylum". Rather it is a place where children may be trained, and the success or failure of the institution is to be judged by the way which it accomplishes this primary purpose.

First comes the training of the body. Since the institution can control the life of the child to a degree impossible or difficult in a boarding home it has an unparalleled opportunity to improve the child's health. It should, of course, have available the necessary medical, dental, and nursing services. The nurse at least should be a resident member of the staff. She can take charge of the infimary and isolation rooms. She can care for the minor ailments of the children and can recognize serious troubles more quickly than an untrained person could and thus refer them to the physician at the earliest possible moment.

The newer knowledge of nutrition has made possible a scientifically balanced diet. The ideal arrangement is to have the purchasing and preparing of food under the care of a trained dietitian. Where this is impossible the menus should be inspected and approved from time to time by an expert. Eating between meals should be discouraged except when a midmorning or mid-afternoon lunch may be found necessary in certain cases.

The institution has a splendid opportunity for training in health habits. Cleanliness of person and belongings should be insisted upon. Each child should have his individual toilet articles which should be kept clean and should not come into contact with those of any other child. The daily routine should allow ample time for sleep including an afternoon nap for the younger children. Each child should be exposed to direct sunlight for some time every sunny day in the year. There should be a special program for undernourished children which should include plenty of rest, plenty of wholesome food, and plenty of light, supervised exercise.

The educational program for the institution should at least reach the standards of a good public school system. In many institutions it is possible to send the children out to a local school. Not only does this relieve the institution of the care of the children's education but it makes for a fuller and more normal life. Since many of the children will be forced to earn their own living at an early age there should be plenty of opportunity for vocational training. Care must be taken, however, that the work which the children do is directed towards their own improvement and does not become merely a method of getting the labor around the institution done cheaply. The range of possible vocations should not be limited to the trades. Children with special ability should have an opportunity to prepare themselves for the higher walks of life and scholarships should be provided for this purpose.

The mental health and character of the children is even more important than their education and physical health. The entering child should be carefully studied from the standpoint of mental hygiene and a plan of treatment should be formulated to correct outstanding faults of character. Not every child can be made an emotionally stable and trustworthy citizen but every child can be helped to greater or less degree by intelligent treatment. The secret of success is to know each child intimately and to make the training suited to his inidividual need. In the more difficult cases the services of a mental-hygiene clinic will be an invaluable aid to diagnosis. The helpfulness of religious training, in such cases, is obvious.

Certain dangers to the child's mental health are inherent in institutional life. One is the lack of a sense of individuality. In the old type of institution the child was swallowed up in a routine which did not distinguish him from the scores or hundreds of children who shared with him the common life. The cottage or group system minimizes this danger but there are certain special methods of meeting it which may be applied even in an old-fashioned institution. One point is to allow the children considerable room for individuality in dress. The old system of marking out the inmates as "orphans" by a special uniform is a subtle cruelty which is now happily passing. Older girls can make or buy their own clothes, thus incidentally receiving an important kind of training. Another device for promoting individuality is to allow each child to have his own possessions and to keep his few toys and trinkets in a special box or locker safe from the other children. A good recreational program, too, will give an opportunity for the development of initiative in the leadership of sports and a well supervised library will help the child to develop its own literary taste.

It is an advantage for the mental health of institutional children if they can be given some contact with the outside world. They should not be made to feel that they are a race apart. Where they go out to school and church this contact is given in a wholesome and natural manner.

Many institutions see no objection in letting their children pass quite freely in and out through the neighborhood. The normal children living at home are able to take care of themselves on the city streets without any very serious physical or moral hazards; there seems to be no reason why the same should not be true of the institutional child.

The child ought to be allowed a small amount of spending money since this affords the only possibility of contact with the economic life of the world around him. Unless some such provision is made there is a grave danger that the institutional child will never acquire the sense of value which comes quite naturally to other children.

It will be necessary naturally to enforce certain rules in the institution. But the most effective discipline is least apparent. In the ideal institution when the children are happy, busy, and healthy, there will be little cause for disciplinary problems to arise. This will be true particularly if the staff has the insight to know the children intimately and the tact to forestall possible outbreaks. Much depends also on having a large enough staff to give individualized attention to each child. Where punishment is necessary it should take the form of deprivation of privileges. In some institutions there is a certain amount of self-government and punishments are inflicted by a board of judges chosen from the children themselves. It is wise to reward merit as well as to punish offenses. The most successful institutions place more emphasis on the former than on the latter.

The religious welfare of the child in the institution is supremely important. Where a child-caring home is under Church control there is an unparalleled opportunity to give such training. This is, in fact, one of the chief arguments in favor of the private institution as opposed to the institution under public control. But even in homes of the latter type arrangements must be made to provide for each child the opportunity to receive religious instruction and to attend Church service. Religion should be the chief force moulding the child's character.

The process of discharge should be given as much attention as the process of admission. The home in which the child is to live, whether it is his own home or not, should be carefully investigated. Very definite plans should be made for the child's education or employment. Some institutions have developed good alumni associations and have encouraged former inmates to return at frequent intervals. By this or some other method an effort should be made to maintain close contact with all the children who have been discharged.

The institution for delinquents presents problems which are different in degree rather than in kind from the usual institution for dependent children (13). In each there must be the same attention to the training and development of personality. As a general thing the population of an institution for delinquents will average older than the population of a home for dependent children. This fact and the fact of the children's delinquency will make the disciplinary problem somewhat more acute but the methods to be followed are much the same.

On the other hand, institutions dealing with children in need of intensive physical care present problems which are not found in an institution for normal children. Under this category are included special homes for cripples, the epileptic, the deaf, and the blind.

The problem of crippled children is being largely solved without institutional care (1). Many cities have special schools or classes for cripples. In some school systems transportation is provided to and from home. In addition to this a number of cities provide for bedside education. After making allowances for these facilities,

however, there will always be a number of cripples who need institutional care either during
a period of treatment in special orthopedic hospitals or convalescent homes or permanently in
institutions for incurable cripples. The institution for these children should contain the special equipment which modern orthopedic work
demands. It should also stress passive recreation
since the treatment is often extremely painful
and everything must be done to keep the children's attention off their troubles.

Epilepsy is a disease which makes its first appearance most frequently in childhood. There
is little hope of effecting a permanent cure in
this disease but progress can be arrested somewhat by a regime which avoids excitement and
involves careful attention to general physical
health. This is secured more easily in an institution or colony than in any system of boarding
homes, the result being that the institution is
society's most common answer to the problem of
epilepsy. Aside from the intensive medical care
and the effort to avoid undue excitement there
is little to distinguish the institution for epileptics from any other institution.

Special homes for the deaf and the blind exist
in nearly all parts of the country. These should
be classed, particularly in the case of the deaf,

as schools rather than child-caring institutions. They endeavor to give the child the specialized training which will enable him to take his place in the world of affairs. In the case of the deaf this will involve training in speech and in lip reading (3). For the blind it will include instruction in reading Braille or some other variety of blind type together with writing, music, vocational education, and physical training (2). A previous chapter has already treated the special problems of institutions for the feeble-minded.

It will be seen from the above that the modern treatment of the dependent and problem child aims to leave him whenever possible in his own home. Where this is impossible an effort is made to provide a boarding home for him in a private family. Institutional treatment is reserved for only those cases in which the other methods are not feasible, and even in institutions an effort is made to preserve something of the spirit of home life. It is thus apparent that the modern care of the dependent child is inspired by an appreciation of the supreme value of home life. The home is Nature's method of rearing the child and it is by attempting to follow in Nature's footsteps that modern child care has achieved its most signal triumphs.

## BIBLIOGRAPHY

(1) Abt, Henry Edward: *The care, cure, and education of the crippled child; a study of American social and professional facilities to care for, cure, and educate crippled children; a complete bibliography of literature bearing on this subject; and a complete directory of institutions and agencies engaged in this work.* Elyria, Ohio, The International Society for Crippled Children, 1924. xi, 222 p.
An account of the problem of the crippled child and the measures being taken for his relief. Very uncritical.

(2) Best, Harry: *The blind; their condition and the work being done for them in the United States.* New York, The Macmillan Company, 1919. xxviii, 763 p.
Although old, this book is valuable as a comprehensive treatment of blindness and the social problems it raises.

(3) Best, Harry: *The deaf; their position in society and the provision for their education in the United States.* New York, Thomas Y. Crowell Company, 1914. xviii, 340 p.
Interesting, though sadly in need of revision.

(4) Evans, Harry C.: *The American poorfarm and its inmates.* Published by The Loyal Order of Moose, Mooseheart, Ill., The Brotherhood of American Yeomen, Des Moines, Iowa, The Maccabees, Detroit, Michigan, The Supreme Tribe of Ben Hur, Crawfordsville, Indiana, The American Insurance Union, Columbus, Ohio, 1926. 119 p.
A careful study of this vanishing institution. Conditions are found to be very bad. Children on the poorfarms have a particularly unhappy lot.

(5) Hart, Hastings H.: *Cottage and congregate institutions for children*. New York, Charities Publication Committee, 1910. xii, 136 p.
A pioneer work. Contains detailed information which will be found interesting even now.

(6) National Conference of Catholic Charities—Sisters' Conference: *A program for Catholic child-caring homes*. Washington, Catholic University of America, 1923. 39 p.
Particularly interesting for its account of the group system.

(7) Reeves, Edith: *Care and education of crippled children in the United States*. New York Survey Associates, 1914. xi, 252 p.
Interesting, though old.

(8) U. S. Bureau of the Census: *Children under institutional care: 1923. Statistics of dependent, neglected, and delinquent children in institutions and under the supervision of other agencies for the care of children with a section on adults in certain types of institutions.* . . . Washington, D. C., U. S. Gov't Printing Office, 1927. 381 p.
This is the fifth federal census on children's institutions. It is the primary source for statistics bearing on the dependent child.

(9) U. S. Bureau of the Census: *Paupers in almshouses, 1923.* Washington, D. C., U. S. Gov't Printing Office, 1925. iv, 76 p.
Of 78,090 paupers in almshouses January 1, 1923 there were 842 (1.1%) under five, 538 (0.7%) between five and nine, and 516 (0.7%) between ten and fourteen.

(10) U. S. Children's Bureau: *Children indentured by the Wisconsin State Public School.* Washington, D. C., U. S. Gov't Printing Office, 1925. v, 132 p. (Children's Bureau Publication No. 150.)

A study of the rapidly vanishing indenture system as applied by a large state institution.

(11) U. S. Children's Bureau: *Handbook for the use of boards of directors, superintendents and staffs of institutions for dependent children.* Washington, D. C. U. S. Gov't Printing Office, 1927. vi, 129 p. (Children's Bureau Publication No. 170.) Probably the best book on modern institutional practice.

(12) U. S. Children's Bureau: *A study of maternity homes in Minnesota and Pennsylvania.* Washington, D. C., U. S. Gov't Printing Office, 1926. v, 92 p. (Children's Bureau Publication No. 167.)
An excellent study.

(13) Van Waters, Miriam: "Where girls go right; some dynamic aspects of state correctional schools for girls and young women." *Survey Graphic* 1:361-76, June, 1922.
A popular exposition of new ideals in this field.

# INDEX

Abbott, G., 105.
Abt, H. E., 281.
Achilles, P. S., 127, 128, 130.
Adoption of Children, 253, 259-60.
Allen, F. J., 213.
American Academy of Political and Social Science, 21.
American Child Health Association, 9, 21, 29, 36, 42, 50, 61, 62, 70, 71, 75, 76, 77, 82.
American Federation of Organizations for the Hard of Hearing, 67, 82.
Army Alpha, 163.
Army Beta, 163.
Association for the Prevention and Relief of Heart Disease, 75-76.

Baden-Powell, R., 186, 193.
Bailey, W. B., 105.
Baker, S. J., 50, 69, 82.
Balch, E., 189.
Barker, L. F., 130.
Beccaria, 88, 89.
Belden, E., 105.
Bernstein, 169-70.
Best, H., 281.
Big Brothers, 104.
Binet, A., 160-62.
Blake, M. B., 213.
Blumenthal, J. L., 69, 82.
Bonser, F. G., 193.
Boy Rangers, 188.
Boy Scouts of America, 194.
Boyce, W. D., 186.
Boys' Club Federation, 188.
Brace, C. L., 247.
Breckinridge, S. B., 21.
Bresnehen, E. L., 213.
Brewer, J. M., 213.

Bridgeport, Conn., Board of Education—Division of Dental Hygiene, 82.
Brill, M. S., 105.
Bronner, A. F., 106.
Brown, S. A., 240.
Bryne, M. E., 172.
Burdge, H. G., 240.
Burt, C. L., 94, 106.
Burtt, H. E., 214.
Byrne, H. A., 241.

Camp Fire Girls, 188.
Camping, 189-90.
Cardiac classes, 75-76.
Carter, W. E., 106.
Castberg, J., 140.
Catholic Boys' Brigade, 188.
Channing, A., 241.
Child-health center, 40-42.
Children's Year, 45.
City-manager plan, 7.
Clark, T., 21, 68-69, 82, 83.
Classical school of penology, 88.
Collins, S. W., 28, 50, 82, 83.
Commission government of cities, 7.
Committee to Study and to Report on the Best Practical Means of Cutting Off the Defective Germ-Plasm in the American Population, 159.
Commonwealth Fund, 108, 115, 123, 125.
Conference of State and Provincial Health Authorities of North America — Standing Committee on Conservation of Vision, 50.
"Congregate type" of child-caring institution, 266.

Kelso, R. W., 22.
Kinder, E. F., 169, 173.
Kite, E. H., 173.
Kitson, H. D., 215.
Klein, A., 83.
Kostir, M. S., 173.

Lane, M. R., 215.
Lee, Joseph, 184, 195.
Lenroot, K. F., 107, 152.
Levy, J., 32, 51.
Lewinski-Corwin, E. H., 44, 51.
Liepmann, M., 107.
Limp, C. E., 215.
Lombroso, 91-92.
Lou, H. H., 107, 132.
Lowe, C., 137, 151.
Lumsden, L. L., 22.
Lundberg, E. O., 23, 107, 108, 134, 151, 261.

McClenahan, B. A., 23.
McGill, N. P., 242.
Magnusson, L., 152.
Marston, L. R., 51.
Maternal mortality, 27.
Maternity centers, 34-36.
Mathews, J. M., 23.
Maxey, C. C., 23.
Mayer, J., 23.
Mental age, 161.
Merritt, E. A., 242.
Metropolitan Life Insurance Company, 51, 110, 132.
Moore, T. V., 132.
Morgan, J. J. B., 132.
Mosher, G. C., 51.
Mothers' pensions, 44, 249-53.
Mulry, T. M., 247.
Murchison, C. A., 108.

"Nams," 158.
Nash, J. B., 195.
National Child Labor Committee, 227, 240, 242.
National Committee for Mental Hygiene, 124-25.
National Conference of Catholic Charities—Sisters' Conference, 282.

National Conference of Charities and Corrections, 247.
National Conference of Commissioners on Uniform State Laws, 141.
National Probation Association, 103-4.
National Research Council, 49.
National Society for the Prevention of Blindness, 75.
Nesbitt, F., 261.
Newark, N. J., Rotary Club, Boys' Work Committee, 195.
Newmayer, S. W., 64, 65, 66, 84.
New York Association for Improving the Condition of the Poor, 65-66.
New York Catholic Charities, 106.
New York Children's Aid Society, 247.
New York Commission on Ventilation, 59.
New York State Commission on Ventilation, 84.
Nursery school, 44-45, 47-49.

Odum, H. W., 24.
O'Grady, J., 261.
Open-air schools, 73-74.
*Ophthalmia neonatorum,* 37.
Oppenheimer, J. J., 132.
Overholser, W., 108.

Paradise, V. I., 242.
Parenthood education, 46-69, 126.
Parsons, P. A., 108.
Peck, M. W., 127, 128, 132, 261.
"Piney's", 158.
Pioneer Youth of America, 188.
Pirquet, C., 51.
Placement of children, 253-60.
Playground and Recreation Association of America, 189.
Pollock, H. M., 133, 173.
Porter, K. H., 24.
Probation, 90, 100-2.
Public Education Association, 123.